Nine Marks of a Good Sermon:

A Guide for Young Preachers

Dwight A. Moody

Academy of Preachers Books

Sarah Kate Bringardner

Actor, Speaker, Coach, Entrepreneur, Friend

and, best of all, Daughter

Contents

Abbreviations for Books Cited

Throughout this book references are made to the five books of sermons published by the Academy of Preachers in partnership with Chalice Press. These sermons were preached at the five National Festivals of Young Preachers, 2010-2014. References to these books will be made by using the following abbreviations:

Beautiful

A Beautiful Thing: Sermons from the Inaugural Festival of Young Preachers, edited by Lee Huckleberry (Chalice Press, 2010)

Waking

Waking to the Holy: Sermons from the 2011 National Festival of Young Preachers, edited by Lee Huckleberry (Chalice Press, 2011)

Uncommon

Uncommon Sense: Jesus and the Renewal of the World, edited by Dwight A. Moody (Chalice Press, 2012)

Gospel

Gospel and the City: Sermons from the 2013 National Festival of Young Preachers, edited by Dwight A. Moody (Chalice Press, 2013)

Questions

Questions of the Soul: Sermons from the 2014 National Festival of Young Preachers, edited by S. Thomas Valentine (Chalice Press, 2014)

Introduction

Christian people deserve to hear good sermons when we gather for worship (or when we download something from the internet). We don't need great sermons, except once in a long while. We hear too many poor or mediocre sermons, and this discourages many people. The church of Jesus Christ is in urgent need of better preaching—and I suspect that has always been the case!

When people in the pew are given the opportunity to comment on their experience at worship, the quality of preaching always receives the most attention. This is true of both Catholic and Protestant preaching. Christians in both traditions testify that preaching is the one element of the worship service most likely to impact both their attendance at the service and their engagement with the worship. Time after time, Christian people report that better preaching is their number one desire when it comes to public worship.

It is no surprise to anyone when I assert that the preaching of the good news about Jesus Christ and the teaching of the Bible are as needed today as ever. When done with competence, preparation, inspiration, and passion, sermons have power to motivate people to faith in God and love toward one another. Good preaching connects people with a power that transforms life. Good preaching shapes personal behavior and public values. Good preaching moves nations to endure hardship, resist evil, and establish justice. Good preaching converts the unbeliever, consoles the burdened, and instructs the eager. Good preaching triggers an exploration of vocation that is at the heart of the call to gospel preaching itself— good preaching begets good preaching!

No preacher is more in need of assistance in preaching than I, and as I have written and taught about preaching, I have sought strategies to improve my own preparation and performance even as I have striven to inspire and instruct others. Out of this mixture of motives have come these homiletic offerings, which I call nine marks of a good sermon. There is nothing original or surprising about the nine marks that I lay out in this short book. I have developed these marks teaching young men and women in a college class on preaching. My students were beginners: full of enthusiasm but, for the most part, lacking in basic public speaking skills. Few knew how to read and study the Bible; fewer knew how to mine its treasures for the instruction and inspiration that constitute the double-barrel whammy of good gospel preaching. Yet every one of them felt called to some sort of public speaking or preaching ministry. Every one of them desired to become a better proclaimer of the good news of Jesus Christ. These nine marks grew out of my desire to respond to this need.

These nine marks arise from no particular theological or denominational preference, although I am a Baptist and thus an heir to one of the great preaching traditions of the modern world. I personally have been influenced by great Baptist preachers such as Charles Haddon Spurgeon, Harry Emerson Fosdick, Billy Graham, Martin Luther King, Jr. and, of course, my own pastors: Clarence Walker, H. C. Chiles, and Walter Price. While in college I heard Ken Chafin preach, and it made a great impression on me. When I stand to preach I hear the words and feel the presence of my theological mentor, Dale Moody. And now, late in life and immersed in the Academy of Preachers, I am listening to seasoned preachers like Dan Boone, Frank Thomas, Alyce McKenzie, and Teresa Fry Brown, and young preachers like Reggie Sharpe AoP'10, Rachel Brocker Langford AoP'12, and Lucas Rice AoP'10. I have learned to hear the voice of God and the call of Christ in many voices, regardless of tradition and style. I give glory to God.

Preachers of all persuasions and of any age need to master these nine marks. Like my students a few years ago, I am intentional in weaving these elements into my sermons. When I sit to prepare a sermon I have this short list by my side and, one by one, ensure that they are fully integrated into my preaching. When I sit in a pew and listen to the preaching of others, I jot this list of nine marks and check them off as the preacher delivers to us what God has laid upon his heart. Using these nine elements will not ensure that the sermon is good—that depends upon other factors such as talent, preparation, and the fundamental content of the message. But when these more basic factors are present in the preacher, integrating these nine marks into a sermon will make her a more effective proclaimer of the distinctive message she is commissioned to preach.

I list these nine in the order that I teach them in my classes, although in reality, they are like the brightly colored horses on a merry-go-round—you can get on any one of them at any time and go the distance! In the same way, any one of these nine marks could be the starting point for preparing or assessing a sermon. But this much is true; week in and week out, the preacher who incorporates these simple elements into a sermon will improve as a communicator of the gospel and do so in a noticeable way. Long ago, the Apostle Paul urged young preachers to work at their craft "so that all may see your progress" (1 Timothy 4:15). Progress in the art and science of preaching is still a desirable trait among ministers of the gospel, and using these simple elements of a good sermon is one way to make progress.

It is also true that as ministers mature, many develop distinctive styles that offer variations of these nine marks. And there are exceptions to every rule, every list. Famous and effective preachers have ignored many of these marks and have had enormous success as preachers. Nevertheless, here is a place to begin for those at the front end of this glorious and burdensome task of making known the mighty wonders of God and the glorious riches that we have in Christ Jesus.

Published here with each of the nine marks is a sermon preached by one of the Young Preachers at one of the first five National Festivals of Young Preachers (and printed in the published book of sermons for that year). These sermons represent the broad spectrum of preaching that occurs at these National Festivals. While each exemplifies one of the nine marks, most contain many of the marks, which I have noted in some places. These sermons were not included here because they were the "best of category," although all of them are good. I have edited each of them for my purposes here, and they are published again with the permission of the Young Preacher. All these sermons can be read in their original form in the book cited, and many are also posted in video on the Academy of Preachers YouTube channel.

Every Good Sermon
Has One Clear Idea

"How many points should a sermon have?" is the setup for an old ministerial joke: "At least one," is the traditional reply. But the sad truth is that many preachers and their listeners are unable to articulate the basic message of the sermon. I certainly have heard many sermons—including some in recent days by seasoned ministers—whose main point I could not identify. More tellingly, I have preached my fair share of sermons that brought this puzzled query from my wife: "What exactly were you getting at today?" Most of these times I failed to clarify in my own mind and on my sermon notes the one, simple point I was trying to make with the sermon.

One clear point is such an elementary rule of public speaking that it almost goes without saying. The recent popularity of the TED Talks has helped remind all public speakers of this simple rule. Coaches tell TED speakers to focus the Talk on the One Big Idea at the center of the 18-minute presentation. Preachers would do well to have such assistance in the preparation of a sermon. Methodist preacher and professor Alyce McKenzie tells of receiving a compliment at the conclusion of a sermon: "Thank you! You only talked about one thing."

To address this idea of simplicity and clarity, many handbooks of preaching require young practitioners to write, often at the top of the sermon manuscript, a thesis or subject sentence. When preachers struggle to identify that sentence, it means two things: first, the preacher is not prepared to preach, or second, the people who hear the sermon will be as confused about its meaning and purpose as the preacher is! It is an injustice to the congregation— and an affront to the gospel itself—for the preacher to be confused about the point and purpose of the sermon.

I recently received a late night phone call from a ministry student. "I have this text," he said, "but the longer I study the more confused and anxious I get." To assist him, I asked: "What is the central idea of your sermon?" He was silent. Then I asked: "What appeal do you want to make?" Again, silence. "Start with these two questions," I recommended; he did, and they proved a way forward in preparing a sermon for the next day!

To reach this place of clarity and simplicity, it is best to avoid those texts or themes that are complicated or touch on several subjects or send the preacher in many directions. Good preachers use rifles rather than shotguns to hit their gospel targets. Preachers like me, especially, who tend in the ADHD direction, need to be aware of this temptation to speak in too many directions and should develop strategies to focus, focus, focus. Some of these strategies might be:

- preaching circles with those who can advise you;

- preaching partners who can listen to your mind and heart and help you focus;

- written sermon thesis and appeal statements;

- use of standard sermon preparation questions that guide you in good directions.

An excellent learning tool is to invite listeners to write or record what they heard as the essential message of the sermon and to compare these with what the preacher intended. Both preacher and people might learn much!

The use of the sermon thesis statement (or appeal statement) is a terrific discipline to develop early. Most sermonic themes can be written as either a declaration or as an exhortation:

- God is merciful;

- Life is a struggle;

- Jesus is alive;

- The Spirit dwells in us.

These are all examples of simple, biblical ideas that are worthy of sermons on a regular basis. Or, if you prefer the appeal or exhortation:

- Trust God;

- Follow Jesus;

- Be constant in prayer;

- Forgive one another;

- Show hospitality.

One clear point is the first rule of preaching, and even experienced preachers need to be reminded of this rule once in a while. It is too easy to get too complicated with a sermon theme. Keep it simple, clear, and focused.

Sermon

Michelle Rushing, AoP'13, preached at the 2014 National Festival of Young Preachers in Indianapolis. She took as her text and theme one of the most famous narratives and questions in the entire Bible: the sacrifice of Isaac with the embedded question, "Where is the lamb for the burnt offering?" She connects this story with one of the central ideas of the Bible: to obey is better than to sacrifice. She uses that assertion as title, message, and conclusion to her sermon, repeating it several times throughout the sermon. It is printed here from the book *Questions* (206-209).

Obedience Is Better Than Sacrifice
Genesis 22:1-7

Close your eyes for a moment. It's morning. The dew is freshly drizzled on the blades of grass as their feet pound the ground. In the silence of the morning, the Lord speaks to Abraham as he and Isaac tread up the side of the mountain. Wretched with anxiety, Abraham feels the tightening in his chest of what is about to happen, but he presses forward because he loves God so much.

Abraham looks down at Isaac for what he feels is the last time, even though his spirit has declared otherwise. Isaac looks up at his father; he smiles not knowing specifically what all of this is about yet trusting his father's lead. Abraham presses on toward the spot where God has deemed this sacrifice to happen. He holds Isaac's hand with firmness and gentleness all at the same time.

As they reach the mountainside, Abraham sees the altar for the offering that he built three days previously. A single tear trickles down his cheek. He wipes it away quickly before Isaac can see it. He wants his son to understand that obedience to God is more important than any human emotion. He thinks the thought, "Obedience is better than sacrifice."

Now open your eyes. Can you imagine the pain and the angst Abraham is experiencing in this passage? Yet in this passage Abraham is recognized for his display of obedience to God. Is obedience better than a sacrifice, even when the sacrifice is dear to you? In the end, God proves this to be true.

God has spoken that Isaac is to be offered up as a burnt offering to test Abraham's obedience. In that time, burnt offerings were symbols of total dedication to God. The offering had to be completely consumed by the fire so that it could be used for nothing else.

I can imagine that Abraham wondered why God would test him with the thing that mattered to him the most. Abraham had waited for the child of the promise, and even in his old age he trusted God, but I wonder if Abraham thought God had gone too far this time.

There are times in our own lives when God asks us to make sacrifices with the things we hold dear. God does not do this to hurt us, but to refocus our attention solely on God. I've thought to myself plenty of times that God had gone too far this time, that God is asking too much of me. But, how successful would you be if God had not asked you offer up to God something of your heart's desire? God tests our obedience in ways that seem harsh to us. God needs to know where our allegiance lies. Even though Abraham was dedicated to God, this one area of his life had the potential to be an idol.

What would cause you to make a hard decision if God asked you to sacrifice it to God?

Abraham was called to be a man of faith. He was walking in his calling. It's when you actually begin to walk in the specifics of what God has called you to do that you have to sacrifice some things. Your sacrifice, much like Abraham's, is not for just you, nor is it just for God. Your sacrifice is so that those around you and those in the kingdom of God see the power of God. The servants that were with Abraham were blessed when they saw Abraham and Isaac come back down the mountain together.

We have to remember that God asks us to give these sacrifices, but God always prepares us for the offering. I lost my car in 2012; it was the one thing that I let define me. I didn't have expensive things or a lot of money in the bank, but I did have a car that I could use as a way to control where my life went.

I remember the moments before it was repossessed. I had talked to the leasing company and had been given some extensions on my payments, but all the while God was preparing me for giving up my car. God was telling me, "I need you to let this go."

The moment I told God that I wanted God's will was the moment I transcended my own human want for obedience to God.

Abraham was very much in the same boat. In chapter 17 of Genesis, God and Abraham make a covenant, and in that moment Abraham activates the very obedience that wills him to take Isaac to the mountain. Although the covenant was geared toward circumcision, it embodied the wholeness of God's need for Abraham.

It's weird to think that God needs us, but it's true. Without the obedience of Abraham, would we have such a graphic example of surrendering to God's will? God has need of your obedience as well; God needs to know that we are willing to put aside our wants for God's will.

You may have to sacrifice the lifestyle you wanted. You may have to sacrifice friendships so that you could grow in some area. You may have to sacrifice your flesh daily in an effort to be a vessel for God.

In the midst of Abraham walking in obedience, we find in verse 3 that he also brought along witnesses; two men came with him to the mountain where the sacrifice would take place. Whenever God asks you to make a sacrifice for God, there will be witnesses. The witnesses are mental scribes who verify the glory of the Lord after the sacrifice has occurred. Abraham was sacrificing a part of himself, and there had to be a witness to that phenomenon. Witnesses carry the fruit of your labor to the fold. I can see the witnesses running back to the town announcing what God had done at the top of the mountain. Your obedience to the anointing of God does not just bring about things for you. There is the example for someone coming after you!

Let's answer Isaac's question, "Where is the lamb for the burnt offering?" The burnt offering is anything that causes you to deny yourself for the sake of being obedient to God. Offering a sacrifice to God is a form of worship. The burnt offering is anything that stands in the way of your destiny with God, anything that has the potential of being an idol. Isaac himself was not a mistake or an idol, but he did have the potential to be one in his father's heart: "You shall not bow down to them or worship them; for I, the LORD your God, am a jealous God" (Exodus 20:5).

Being jealous is defined as feeling or showing suspicion of someone's unfaithfulness in a relationship. This word usually has a negative connotation, but when it is coupled with the divine, it expresses the seriousness of our relationship with God.

Whenever God calls us to be obedient, there is always a grace note. God will spare the very thing you were so willing to sacrifice for God. When God sees that you chose the divine over that thing, God's hand acts in your favor.

We know the rest of the story. God sends the angel to stop Abraham from killing Isaac. Isaac was merely the instrument, or the catalyst, for God's glory. To answer the question again, the burnt offering is the very thing that will bring God glory! The sacrifice will press you further into your calling and your destiny. Isaac was the very thing that pushed Abraham further into his faith call.

When God sees that you will give up your prized possessions and the things that you hold so dear just to see God's glory, God wastes no time coming to your rescue. "Jesus said to her, 'Did I not tell you that if you believed, you would see the glory of God'" (John 11:40).

The good news is that your obedience genuinely and specifically empowers the hand of God. In verse 10, Abraham is committing the very act of obedience. In verse 11, God sees the epic seriousness of Abraham's obedience in such a way that it proves to God that Abraham's obedience is more important to Abraham than the sacrifice!

Abraham teaches us that the sacrifice itself is not what's important, but it is the very act of obedience. Obedience is better than the sacrifice.

Every Good Sermon
Arises Naturally from a Biblical Text

To "take a text" is, in some Christian traditions, a euphemism for preaching—"Rev. Jones took a text today" is the same as saying "Our preacher today was Rev. Jones." There is good reason for this phrase:

- Good preaching is connected to the Bible from start to finish.

- Good preaching takes its inspiration and its message from the Bible.

- Good preaching shows evidence of constant dialogue with the vast range of materials in the Bible.

To contend that a sermon must be connected to a biblical text is, of course, overstatement; there are actually many wonderful sermons with no apparent connection to the Bible. This is especially true when the audience does not recognize the Bible as the Word of God. When the Apostle Paul preached in Athens, as recorded in Acts 17, he quoted not the Hebrew Scriptures (which he normally did when speaking in Jewish synagogues) but two Greek poets and one funeral inscription. Every preacher will find opportunities to speak good news to audiences not accustomed to biblical exposition or even biblical reference. This is the difference between parish preaching, where the audience is the Christian community, and public preaching, where the audience is the broader human community. Examples of public preaching often include funerals, weddings, civic gatherings, and radio, television, and internet preaching.

But for most preachers these public preaching events are exceptions to the general rule; parish preaching is more the norm. Congregations of Christian people who gather to worship desire to have the words of the preacher connected to the Word of God, and this is best accomplished by taking a text.

Whole books have been written on this rule of preaching, and I have no intention of summarizing the common arguments for its centrality. I simply have it as a guide for young preachers that you take a biblical text and study the text, so that when you preach, you explain what the text means to us today. Preachers are always tempted to settle on a preaching theme, then search for a text to support a message; others take a text and read into its words things that never were there and should not be there. Learning how to read and interpret the biblical text is a first discipline of good preaching.

This, of course, is a major justification for education—for as much education as you can get! Knowing the history of the Bible, the interpretation of the Bible in the long history of the church, the languages of the Bible and the customs of the biblical times: these are invaluable in preparing to preach. Excavating both the theology of a text and the sociology of a congregation require a level of learning that does not come naturally and without work. In fact, both of these tasks are lifelong pursuits, and attention to them will keep your preaching fresh and your discernment rich.

Many preachers find a great help in using a plan of biblical texts, such as the lectionary. Many religious traditions use lectionaries, which are lists of sacred texts designed to be read in certain ways on certain days. These are arranged, not randomly, but in accordance with events and themes. All preachers can at least try this way of sermon preparation, even if you either occasionally depart from it or eventually abandon it in favor of other methods of connecting sermons with scripture. Another method is to take portions of scripture—whole books of the Bible or sections of the Bible, such as the Sermon on the Mount or the life of David—and use these week by week as a basis for preaching. Yet another way is to select a theme, such as forgiveness, or failure, or fear, and locate biblical texts that serve to explicate the meaning and relevance of what the Bible has to say. All of these are excellent ways to systematically connect the sermon with the biblical witness.

But there is this: the Bible is a complicated and sometimes confusing book. It contains many kinds of literature, some of which lend better to preaching than others. I recommend that you as a young preacher use familiar texts that support a single theme, such as Genesis 1 (creation), Psalm 23 (trust), and I Corinthians 13 (love). Use also those that touch upon the great themes and questions of the spiritual life: themes like despair and hope, friendship and forgiveness, or courage and fear. I once heard Billy Graham take Psalm 102:6 as a text: "I am like an owl in the wilderness, like a pelican in the desert" (KJV) and preach a memorable sermon on loneliness. The power of that simple biblical metaphor and the simplicity of the sermon impressed me then and lingers with me to this day.

Experienced preachers and teachers will be able to handle difficult texts and troubling issues in more appealing and powerful ways than a beginner, and they will also be able to draw out of the texts the mysteries, the contractions, and the challenges to our presuppositions and preferences. But learning to preach, like learning to play the piano, will be aided if you keep to texts that are familiar and straightforward.

Sermon

When he was a student at St. Johns University, **Cody Maynus**, AoP'10, preached at the inaugural Festival of Young Preachers in Louisville. He took as his text the wonderful assertion in the prologue of John's gospel, "The Word Became Flesh," and he stuck right to it through this sermon, entitled "That Liberating Word." It was published in *Beautiful* (56-59). I present it here because it illustrates this mark of a good sermon: take a text and let it speak.

The Word Became Flesh
John 1: 1-18

The Word became flesh. What a fantastic notion! Savor it! The Word became flesh. Thank about it. The Word—Jesus the Christ—became flesh—a human being. Internalize it. The Word—Jesus the Christ, the savior of humanity and the son of God the Creator—became flesh—a human being who experienced hunger and desire. The notion that an omnipotent God—the Creator of the Heavens and the Earth—would come down to this dirty, hell-hole of a world, assume humanity and become one of many of God's creatures is either radical or ridiculous.

This definitely radical and perhaps ridiculous notion is the central element of Christianity. Two thousand years of ecclesiastical history can be traced back to one event: the Incarnation, the moment when the Creator became the created.

If we were to look at the Incarnation from the non-Christian perspective, we would see something very strange. We would see a potter becoming one of his pots. We would see a painter become one of her paintings, a child becoming one of his sandcastles. Why would a Creator God become one of said Creator God's creations? It doesn't make sense, does it? In the person of Jesus Christ, God took on humanity so that God could liberate humanity.

The writer of the Gospel according to John tells us several things about Jesus. Of the many things we are told, we are told that Jesus is life and that this life was humanity's light. Can you image the world that Jesus was born into? Jesus was a Jew. He was born into poverty. He was born into a people living under imperial oppression. He was born into a people who have been waiting for a savior for hundreds of years. Jesus the Christ is the Anointed One, the Messiah, the Savior of these people. He is their light and he comes to se them free from their own darkness.

For those of you who may not celebrate the liturgical calendar in your faith tradition, Christmas comes after the season of Advent— four weeks of waiting, hoping, and praying that the Messiah—the Anointed One, the Savior—would one day come. During Advent those of us in the liturgical traditions light candles that represent the Light of the World—Jesus Christ, the Word of God who was made flesh. As the College of St. Benedict, where I am a minister of spirituality and social justice, we celebrated Advent with the community for 200 or so Benedictine nuns, professors, and students. Our chapel is absolutely gorgeous with wonderful neo-gothic architecture which leaves the chapel quite dark unless lit by electric lights.

During an evening worship service toward the end of Advent we turned off all the electric lights in the chapel, leaving only the four pillar candles surrounding the altar lit and providing illumination for the crowd. As the scripture was read for the evening—this very scripture that I am preaching from now—a group of nuns and students took small candles, lit them on the altar candles, and moved throughout the congregation sharing light with each person. By the time the lector got to the part of the reading where is says, "The light shines in the darkness, and the darkness did not overcome it" (John 1:5) all of our candles were lit.

The group assembled that evening were very much representative of humanity. We were men and women, young and old, students and professors. We were European, Asian, African, and Native descent. We were Christian, Jewish, Buddhist, Agnostic, Wiccan. We were rich and poor, wise and foolish. We were future theologians, scientists, authors, teachers, politicians, lawyers, doctors, nuns, criminals. We were the people who will be sitting in your pews one day. We were representative of all facets of humanity. It was for us that God became a human in the person of Jesus the Christ.

The scripture does not say, "the life was the light of Catholics" or "the life was the light of white people." No, the gospel says that the life was the light of humanity, of all humanity. Again, this is a radical notion! It is really radical to think that a magnificent and awe-inspiring God would enter into humanity to save us, even the human who may not be getting it just right or may not be pretty or smell nice or able to recite the Creeds or quote scripture or solve algorithms or tie shoes or even possess shoes to tie.

It is important for us to examine the conditions of the Incarnation. The Incarnation happens in a specific way during a specific time and at a specific place. Logically, the incarnation could have happened ten or fifteen years ago, in the fanciest of hospitals, with the wealthiest of parents, and the salvific results would have been the same. Humanity would have been reconciled to its Creator.

Salvation would have occurred. Heaven's gate would have been open wide. Jesus would still have been the Son of God, the Messiah, the Anointed One, the Savior. But it did not happen 10 or 15 years ago in a fancy hospital to wealthy parents. In fact, it happened 2,000 years ago in a stinky barn to a teenage woman and her fiancée. Why? What is the importance of the Incarnation happening under those circumstances?

The early church historian, St. Iranaeus, explains the Incarnation by saying, "The Word of God, Jesus Christ, out of his boundless love, became what we are that he make us what he is." Jesus because became what we are so that we could become what he is!

Ahah! Therein resided the reasoning behind the Incarnation happening in a specific time and place in history.

If one reads this section of the Gospel with a copy of the Magnificat of Mary, one can see the distinct social message that the Gospel is trying to present. In her song, Mary sings of God lifting up the poor and throwing down the rich. She sings of the oppressed being liberated. Jesus is the example of the oppressed being raised and liberated. It is evident, given the Magnificat and the life of Jesus as shown throughout the Gospels, that God was very purposeful in scheduling and working the events leading to the Incarnation. God selected a poor, unmarried woman to bear the Savior of the World. God selected a people living on the fringes of society—a people whom the Romans look upon as weird for the dress, cuisine and religious practices. Jesus connects with those who reside on the fringes of our society.

- Christ is the immigrant man who works two shifts at the factory.

• Christ is the young woman who may not preach because of her gender.

• Christ is the gay man who may not marry his committed partner.

• Christ is the piece seamstress who may not sit down on a bus.

• Christ is the Buddhist who is trying to make sense of life in a Christian world.

• Christ is the pacifist who seeks to proclaim a Gospel on nonviolence.

This is who Christ is. By the incarnation, we are made to be like these people. We are made to be the people, the churches, and the communities of Christ. In doing so, we are liberated from the bondages of human darkness. Jesus Christ is the candle that brings light to our dark, cold world. Jesus Christi is our Savior. Amen.

Every Good Sermon Responds to the Needs of the People

Much has been written recently about the pros and cons of need-based preaching, need-based evangelism, and need-based church programming. Need-based ministry has been quite a trend in recent decades, and congregations have spawned program upon program to follow through on the need-based empathy that dominates many pulpits. Speaking to the felt needs of people has been a key element in the growth and influence of many congregations. In this vein, preachers have taken up themes like:

- Surviving and thriving during failure

- Seven rules for a stronger marriage

- Strategies for resisting temptation and overcoming sin

These are important themes, of course, and give occasion for the gospel preacher to bring the good news of Jesus Christ to the life experiences of people. People need help in coping with failure, marriage, and temptation. This attention to the social, emotional, and spiritual needs of the people is an essential component of effective preaching of the gospel.

Need-based anything can be overdone, of course. We can end up simply catering to the whims and desires of people, of indulging our self-centeredness, of intensifying the fundamental disease of our "me-first" culture. There are many examples of this in every corner of our culture, including religion; in fact, what is known as the Prosperity Gospel has overtaken much of the Christian community, in America and around the world. It promises that faithful, holy living will result in physical, social, and financial success, a notion far from the message of the Lord Jesus Christ who lived without home or family and died without justice or success.

But sermons that do not connect in some way with the hopes and despairs of the people, with the grit and glory of life as it is being lived by the people, with the victories and defeats of those who sit in the congregation—sermons that do not connect with this, with these needs, will fail to move and comfort and warn and instruct. In reality, all successful leadership and ministry has addressed the needs of an audience or congregation. This is why pastoral care, which is a form of professional listening, is essential to competent preaching. When speaking to committees seeking an interim pastor I frequently point out how pastoral contact with the congregation is needed even by interim preachers in order to make the Sunday sermon useful in the life of the church.

In the midst of national struggle or turmoil, people need to hear a word about the sustaining power of God "who is with you always to the end of the age" (Mathew 28:20) or about the call for people to rise above self-interest to "strive first the kingdom of God" (Matthew 6:33). After a local teenager dies in an automobile accident, people need to experience the comfort of God expressed through friendship, service, and worship, as described by the Apostle Paul in his appeal to Christians "to console those who are in any affliction with the consolation with which we ourselves are consoled by God" (2 Corinthians 1:4). When an ethnic community is transplanted into the ministry field of a congregation, people need to be reminded of the ministry of hospitality as expressed in the words of Jesus, "For I was a stranger and you welcomed me" (Matthew 25:35). These and a thousand more life situations come up unexpectedly to a Christian congregation, and the preacher has the wonderful opportunity to bring to bear on such dilemmas the mercy and grace of God as reflected in the life of our Lord. Jesus himself, you recall, dealt with empire and taxes, food and clothing, friendship and forgiveness, and success and failure. Jesus discerned the needs of people and addressed them in public and in private. No wonder they heard him gladly (Mark 12:37).

It is tempting for ministers to preach to and from our own needs, thinking that the issues and episodes that roil our own souls are also burning down the barns where our people live and work. I have done this often, especially early in my ministry. I look back and bemoan the lost opportunities to bring the gospel to bear upon the things that matter most to those who heard me preach. I was so caught up in my own world of ideas and issues that I failed to understand and appreciate the situations and struggles of my people. This is a deadly sin, to the preacher and to the congregation.

Here are a few practical ways to keep attuned to the needs of your people.

      • Read the news, watch the news, and keep up with what is happening.

      • Visit in the homes and workplaces of your people.

- Communicate with your people, especially via social media.

- Provide ways for your people to provide feedback about your preaching and their lives.

- Ask your people what they want addressed by the preacher.

And keep in mind this old question often put to professors: "What do you teach?" The expected answer is physics or language or history; but the truest answer is, students: "I teach students." Likewise, a preacher focuses primarily not on ideas, or texts, or even truths, but people. We preach to people and for people, and knowing them well makes our preaching rich, relevant, and rewarding.

Sermon

Johannes Duckeck, AoP'12, was a student at Cincinnati Christian University when he came to Louisville for the 2012 National Festival of Young Preachers. The preaching theme that year was "The Sermon on the Mount," and Johannes took as his text that part of the Sermon on the Mount where Jesus calls us not to worry but to trust God in all things, at all times. His sermon, "Got Worries? God Helps!" arises from the common needs of students especially and issues a strong appeal for us to trust God in times of need. It is published in the book *Uncommon* (180-184).

Got Worries? God Helps!
Matthew 6:25-34

"I need to read a book, write a review, figure out a topic for my research paper, and prepare the lesson for Bible study. My shift at the coffee shop doesn't start until 9 tonight, so I have some time. Then there is Annabelle: I need to buy some groceries for the dinner with her. I want to impress her when I cook for her tomorrow. What should I wear? I need to look good. I will work on the research paper later tonight. I know it is due Friday. I don't know if I'll have time for my devotions. I hope I don't forget to go to the library for some resources. What if I get a bad grade on this paper? I might fail that class. Or even worse: what if Annabelle doesn't like my cooking. Oh, my phone is vibrating. I need to take this call."

That is some kind of stress. So many worries!

Can you identify with that?

There are so many things that cause us to worry. That might be a typical college students list of things but all of us worry: that project not done; that new boyfriend your daughter seems to like; your social security projections; or the uncertainties of getting older.

Sometimes we forget about God in all this. Our worry leads us away from God. We need to work on these things, make preparations for them, plan them out. Our time with God grows smaller and smaller. We fail to meditate in the morning because we are too busy. We do not take advantage of the worships events around us. God is pushed into the background by our daily worries. Our worry leads us away from God, but with the right perspective, they can lead us to God!

We are not the first people to worry. Anxiety is as old as humanity. Even the people in the Bible times were worried. Jesus addressed this in the Sermon on the Mount. "Therefore I tell you, do not worry about your life, what you will eat or drink, or about your body, what you will wear. Is not life more important than food, and the body more important than clothes? ...Therefore do not worry, saying 'What shall we eat?' or 'What shall we drink?' or 'What shall we wear?'.... Indeed your heavenly Father knows that you need all these things. But strive first for the kingdom of God and his righteousness, and all these things will be given to you as well. So do not worry about tomorrow, for tomorrow will bring worries of its own. Today's trouble is enough for today. (Matthew 6:25, 31-34)

Jesus says three things about worry. First, worry doesn't get us anywhere. Who of us by worry can add a single year to our lives? Worry leads to nothing. We become anxious. Anxiety paralyzes. Anxiety about this sermon is one of the worst things I can do because it will actually keep me from doing it.

Think how much time we waste picking out the right clothes when the important thing is just that we wear something. How futile our attempts at controlling all these things!

Looking at nature shifts our perspective. God is there in nature and God provides for the birds and flowers. Nothing we ever do can match God's care for his creation. Jesus mentions Solomon, the richest king in Israel's history. He had everything! But it wasn't the same as God's care for the flowers.

If we seek these things, we make it obvious how stuck we are in this world. The world worries; awe should not be like the world. Worry is worldly. By worry, the world seeks to control things. It's not just about controlling things; it is about having things. Jesus said: "Do not store up for yourselves treasure on earth, where moth and rust consume and where thieves break in and steal; but store up for yourselves treasures in heaven, where neither moth nor rust consumes and where thieves do not break in and steal. For where your treasure is, there your heart will be also" (Matthew 6:19-21).

This is why we should not worry. Worry leads us to control everything. We think about all the things we need to control. Michael Jackson was successful and rich. But he worried that he wasn't going to be happy enough, so be bought all things of things to distract himself. Later in life he became extremely worried about his health. It didn't get him anywhere.

The world has no solutions to our worries. Listen to the words of this classic song:

> Hakuna matata—what a wonderful phrase
>
> Hakuna matata—ain't no passing craze.

It means no worries for the rest of your days.

It's a problem-free philosophy!

Hakuna matata.

This happy tune is from the movie *The Lion King*. But it is not always that easy. We cannot stop worry on our own. With God's help we can. Jesus tells us what to do. "Strive first for God's kingdom and his righteousness and all these other things will be given to you as well" (Matthew 6:33).

Seek God first. God will take care of us. We can't let our worries overwhelm us! God has promised to care for us. God knows our needs. God will provide for us.

Our esteemed professor Dan Dyke tells the story of the early years of his marriage. He was still in school. He often did not know how the money would suffice for school, house and food. He tells of one instance when he and his wife actually ran out of food. The pantry was empty; there was nothing left. They thought they would have to go hungry before the next paycheck. But that very day, his wife found a $20 bill in the street! God provides for his people!

We still have a responsibility. We cannot take God's provision as an excuse to do nothing. Our trust should not turn to apathy!

As I was preparing this sermon, I just told myself "This is going to work out..." and went to play a video game. That is not right. It also doesn't mean we can be careless with our money, buying a large TV and a gaming system, thinking, "God will take care of our school bills."

Dr. Dyke did not use his money carelessly. He simply did not have very much at all.

God provides! God provides not only in these situations of little, daily worries, but also for our ultimate worry: "What happens after death?"

God sent Jesus to this Earth, to live among us, to minister to us, to tell us not to worry but shift our focus back to God. God sent Jesus to die for us on the cross so that we do not to be worried about death. We are accepted by grace to live in eternity with God!

What we need to do is seek God first. Not doing your morning meditation in favor of homework is a terrible idea! Taking opportunity to worship or serve despite feeling overwhelmed by workload can be an extremely rich experience. God will bless you and assure you of God's presence.

With the assurance that God is going to provide for us, that God's going to look after us, that God knows of our needs and will supply them, we can calm down. We can approach things without so much worry.

Calm down and seek God. Seek God in prayer. Seek God in other people. Seek God in your work. Remember: God sought you first. God sent Jesus. God wants to be there for you. Allow God to provide. Take courage! God is there! God knows your needs. God will supply your every need.

Every Good Sermon Includes a Story

The Bible is full of stories, and this is a good pattern for all gospel preachers. Genesis opens the biblical narrative with the story of creation; and Revelation closes it with the extended story of the triumph of God. From cover to cover, the Word of God comes to us in stories.

- The great flood and the tower of Babel

- The sacrifice of Isaac and flight of Jacob

- The exodus from Egypt and the conquest of the Land

- The birth of Samuel and the anointing of David

- The destruction of Jerusalem and the rebuilding of the wall

- The birth and baptism of Jesus

- The arrest and trial of Paul

The birth of Jesus may be the most widely known story in the world; if not, it is second only to the story of his resurrection. The life of Jesus is primarily a series of stories strung together to make some theological point about God and God's purpose in the world. This is precisely the basic strategy of gospel preaching: use stories to say something about God and God's purpose in the world.

People like stories, which is why they dominate most conversations: in church and out of church, at home and away from home, in books, on television and at the theater. Stories are the stuff of human life, and the gospel preacher will spend her life gathering stories, telling stories, and interpreting stories in order to say something true about life and death, truth and error, courage and fear, love and hate. During my lifetime, the mega-stories of *Star Wars, Star Trek, Narnia*, Middle-earth, *Harry Potter*, superheroes (Superman, Batman, etc.), and the *Hunger Games* have dominated the imaginations of entire generations of readers and viewers.

Miles Holt, AoP'13, was a student at Mercer University when he came to preach at the 2013 National Festival of Young Preachers. He carefully sliced in two the powerful story of Jean Valjean in Victor Hugo's *Les Miserables*. He began his sermon as the novel does, with the narrative of mercy shown by Monsignor Charles Francois-Bienvenu Myriel, and concluded the sermon with the other episode of mercy shown by Jean Valjean as he carried Marius to safety through the underground sewers of Paris. It is hard to undermine the impact of such stories, and they are best told straightforward and without ornamentation. (*Gospel*, 91-94)

Jesus told stories; stories are powerful avenues of communicating whatever is true and useful and of good report. People are more apt to remember a good story than any other part of the sermon. So why would any preacher neglect to tell a story? Yet many do, but I insist on this—that every sermon include a story. It can be a biblical story and often should be; our people are very ignorant of the Bible, and great good can come from simply telling from the pulpit the stories of the Bible. A student once approached me about preaching about Nicodemus but could not "find the handle" of a sermon. "Just tell the story," I advised, "all three acts of the Nicodemus drama in the gospel of John. Do not assume your people know the story, let alone what inspiration might be drawn from it."

The story of a sermon can also come from the public experience, of war or tragedy or danger or despair. Stories from the civil rights struggle or a political campaign or a Super Bowl season are in the public realm and make for compelling rhetoric. Movies, books, magazines, television, conversation, even songs are wonderful resources for stories. Constance Cherry, noted preacher and writer on worship, used a famous Nazi death-camp story from Corrie Ten Boom's book *The Hiding Place*[1] to make a memorable sermon during the 2014 National Festival of Young Preachers. You can read that sermon in the book *Questions* (269-275) and also watch it on the AoP YouTube channel.

But many stories worth telling are those connected with your own experience. I have often told the stories of running away from school on the very first day of first grade, of sitting in a courtroom while a judge sentenced my son to 93 months in federal prison, and of surviving not one, not two, but three death-defying automobile accidents. While there is much debate on how often and how thorough such autobiographical material should be employed in the preaching ministry, this much is sure: testimony is a powerful element of any public speaking. More than once, Paul the apostle

---

[1] Peabody, Massachusetts: Hendrickson Publishers, 2009

stood before a hostile audience and told the story of his conversion to Christ (Acts 9:1-19, 22:1-21, 24:10-21, 26:1-29). It was compelling then and is compelling now.

Being alert and open to stories that come to us through media, that are embedded in our own history, and that greet us in the ebb and flow of our own daily activities is an essential skill of the preacher. At the 2015 National Festival of Young Preachers in Dallas, plenary preacher Joel Gregory made a plea for just this type of gospel attention to what we see and hear and experience all around us.

> Sometimes you are on your way to the best of stories, and you don't even know it. Let me give you a hint: when you are on your way to something big in preaching, a story that is just right, heaven doesn't open and a big [voice] doesn't say "Now here it is." The best stories are those things that come to your life by a divine synchronicity, and you're not just telling that story; that story becomes part of you.

Gregory, of course, is the master of that, and his just-quoted sermon illustrates that well; and you can watch it on the AoP YouTube channel.

This much is true: any sermon is made better by the inclusion of a good story; and good sermons come close to greatness when they include a good story well told. Sometimes, more than we wish to admit, simply telling a story is sufficient for preaching what our people need and want to hear. Jesus did it, and so can we.

Sermon

Here is a sermon by **Chris Hughes**, AoP'11, who has preached at several National Festivals of Young Preachers. When he came to Atlanta in January of 2013, he was a third-year student at Wake Forest Divinity School in North Carolina. This sermon illustrates wonderfully how to weave together three stories: a biblical story (of Jonah), a personal story (of his own baptism), and the story of another (the conversion of Anne Lamott). His sermon, "Salvation in Unexpected Places" is also found in *Gospel* (95-99).

Salvation in Unexpected Places
Jonah 2:4-9

I was 10 years old when I made my first profession of faith. My brother had been baptized just one year earlier, and I decided that I, too, was ready: ready to make on the call to faith and ready to follow Jesus. My pastor required that I meet with him to talk it over, and so I did, on a Sunday night just a few weeks before I wanted to be baptized. I talked though every bit of the Christian talk that I knew, that I was a sinner in need of God's saving grace and that I needed to believe and baptized. Then he looked right at me and asked the questions: "Do you really know what this means?"

The question haunts me still. Dow e ever really know what God's grace means? Even when we think we have it figured out, isn't there still so much to amaze about the way God redeems? Does grace only come to us once? Or can grace find its way into our lives in all kinds of places and all kinds of times and all kinds of people, even in ways we least expect?

Redemption and salvation are at the heart of the Johan story. It is a strange tale of the gospel in an even stranger city. Jonah makes for a peculiar prophet. He does nothing right. He is never called a prophet and never speaks in oracles. He is not sent to the people of Israel but to the foreign city of Nineveh. Instead of a mouthpiece for God he is grumbling, pouty and short spoken. The Jonah story is God working through our comedy of errors to tell a salvation story.

"Go at once to Nineveh, that great city and cry against it; for their wickedness has come before me" (Jonah 1:2). God's call comes clearly and simply; yet Johan resists. Yahweh called him to go east, to Nineveh, but he goes west, to Tarshish.

Jonah "fled from the presence of God," the Bible says. Don't we all flee from time to time? Whether it was before we hitched onto the grace wagon or after, don't we occasionally fall off? We feel the call of God to go, to preach, t help, to be transformed; and instead, we find every reason why we shouldn't, why we couldn't. Instead of taking the gospel call out into the neighborhoods, into the cities, to the everyday people we encounter, we stand there stammering like Moses. Jonah fled, too, wherever he could go and whatever the cost.

Jonah finds the first ship out of town, hops on board, and thinks he's made a quick getaway. He learns, however, that God's call can follow you. God sends a great storm. The wind howls and tears across the sea, the waves crash over the bow, the creaking ship seems like it will break at any moment. The crew is in hysterics, and after a little nap, Jonah confesses: "I'm the one to blame; thrown me out so the storm will end" (Jonah 1:12, paraphrased).

Was he being heroic? Or did he think his time had really come? Either way, they do the dirty deed and when he's gone, the sailors "fear the Lord." Jonah wins his first convert without saying a word.

God's not done yet.

God finds a fish, makes him swallow down the hapless, wondering Jonah. And here, God does the difficult inner work of redemption. Jonah has time to think about what all he's done, what God's done, and what he's going to do now. For three day, he sits and thinks. Now begins the long road to transformation. It begins with a plea, a song a thanksgiving.

I call to the Lord out of my distress, God answered me:

> *I called to the Lord out of my distress, and he answered me;*
> *Out of the belly of Sheol I cried, and you heard my voice….*
> *The waters closed in over me…, weeds were wrapped*
> *around my head….*
>
> *Yet you brought up my life from the Pit, O Lord my God.*
> *As my life was ebbing away, I remembered the Lord,*
> *And my prayer came to you…,but I with the voice of*
> *thanksgiving will sacrifice to you…. Deliverance belongs to*
> *the Lord.* (Jonah 2:1-9)

In the depths of the sea and in deepest distress, Jonah senses the grace of God, and he comes to his senses. Isn't it a wonderful that in those moments when we felt furthest from the grace of God, it shows up in surprising ways?

God showed up to Anne Lamott in the unlikeliest of ways. She was becoming a successful West Coast writer, but her life meandered this way and that because of drugs, alcohol, and broken relationship. She writes: "I did not mean to be a Christian. My first words upon encountering the presence of Jesus for the first time a few years ago were 'I would rather die.'"[2] She continues in her book *Traveling Mercies*[3]:

> I really would have rather died at that point than
> to have my wonderful, brilliant, left-wing, non-
> believer friends know that I had begun to love
> Jesus. I think they would have been less appalled if
> I had developed a close personal friendship with
> Strom Thurmond ... . I didn't experience[3] [Jesus]
> so much as the hound of heaven, as the old
> description has it, as the alley cat of heaven, who
> seemed to believe that if it just keeps showing up,
> mewing outside your door, you'd eventually open
> up and give him a bowl of milk (49).

Lamott found herself in desperate times. After having an abortion, she spent an entire week in a stupor from drugs and loss of blood. She found Jesus then, sitting in the corner one night "on his haunches ... watching ... with patience and love." She thought it was her imagination but everywhere she went thereafter, she seemed to feel the cat nipping at her heels.

Lamott made her way to her funky little church, the one she had come to know as a second home, and it was there that it happened, during the last hymn. "It was as if the people were singing in between the notes. I felt like their voices or something was rocking

---

2 "Spiritual Chemotherapy," in Salon.com, February, 1997, p. 3
3 *Traveling Mercies: Some Thoughts on Faith* (New York: Anchor, 2000)

me in its bosom, holding me like a scared kid, and I opened up to that feeling and it washed over me."

She began crying and left before the benediction, running all the way home, and there she found Jesus waiting for her. "Oh, all right," she said, letting out a long sigh, "you can come in." One found redemption in the belly of a fish, another in the final pains of losing her child.

There's more salvation to be found. The whale gets indigestion, vomits our prodigal prophet onto the beach, and Jonah finally goes to Nineveh. He's changed, somewhat. It takes three days to walk throughout Nineveh; and what do you know, Jonah goes only one day into the streets preaching this message, "Forty days and Nineveh is toast." He plops down outside the city on a stump, waiting to see the fireworks.

Here the story takes its biggest turn. The whole town repents! News spreads and the kind gets involved. "Everything is to put on sackcloth and ashes!" declares the king. "Did he say everything?" Yes, everything, even the women and children, even the cows and sheep. Maybe God will change God's mind, they think.

And God Does! God repents, the King James Version says. A *metanoia*, a turning, is happening in the mind and heart of God. Seeing the change in the people of that city, god is transformed as well.

What a story! Despite all this half-hearted efforts, all the people whom Jonah thought were too far off from God to be saved, to find grace and goodness, find it. They understand it even better than he does. Perhaps that's the point. Jonah, stubborn as a mule, thinks he knows where grace is and to whom it belongs. But God is out to shatter our notions of grace, to make them bigger and broader, to include everyone everywhere.

Our hearts can be changed and cause us to love people we once thought unlovable. Grace can show up in ways we thought impossible, even in the places we never dreamed it would happen. God called Jonah to the great city of Nineveh, and everything changed because of it.

"Salvation belongs to the Lord!" We don't know why or how, but it happens it us.

- Grace comes to the woman standing in line at the food bank.

- Grace comes to the gay couple finally allowed to marry.

- Grace comes to the children making wages chipping gravel.

- Grace comes to your friends and to your enemies.

Finally, our story concludes. God makes one last try to put things in perspective for Jonah. God gives Jonah a shady tree to sit under. But Jonah gripes still. "I knew you are a gracious God and merciful, slow to anger, and abounding in steadfast love. Why did I even come here? I'd rather die than live in a world where these people don't get what they deserve!" Jonah still does not understand the mercy of God. So God kills the tree, and Jonah pouts all the more. God delivers the last unsettling questions. "You love this tree though it was here today and gone tomorrow. Can I not also love everything I have created: everything, even the thousands of people living in Nineveh, even the animals?"

Everything? Yes, everything.

Every Good Sermon
Includes a Question

I once designated a Bible as my "Question Bible." As I read through that Bible, I underlined (and counted) every question. There are approximately 2,550 questions in the NRSV of the Protestant version of the Scriptures. Most surprising to me was the number of questions in the Psalms:

What are human beings that you are mindful of them? (8:4)

- How long, O Lord? (13:1)

- Why have you forsaken me? (22:1)

- Where can I go from your spirit? (139:7)

It is not surprising how many questions occur on the lips of Jesus.

- Which one of these three was a neighbor to the man? (Luke 10:36)

- Did the baptism of John come from heaven? (Matthew 21:25)

- Why are you afraid? (Mark 4:40)

- Why do you not understand what I say? (John 8:43)

The Sermon on the Mount has no fewer than 21 question marks! Jesus knew that few things are as powerful as a question: as the title, as the introduction, as a transition, as a conclusion.

These biblical questions offer a wealth of preaching material. In fact, throughout 2013 and including our National Festival of Young Preachers in January of 2014, we used 52 of these questions as our preaching texts for our Academy of Preachers events. Here are some of the questions on that list:

- Have you only one blessing? (Genesis 27:38)

- What do people gain from all their toil? (Ecclesiastes 1:3)

- Son of Man, can these bones live? (Ezekiel 37:3)

- Who will separate us from the love of God? (Romans 8:35)

At the end of that year we published a book entitled *Questions of the Soul.* It contains 64 sermons, all but two by young preachers.

The wise preacher will often pull from these biblical questions for his sermons. In fact, it might be a smart thing to do an annual series of questions. There are enough questions straight out of the Bible to keep a preacher in fine sermonic shape for years!

Then there are the questions people ask, questions that arise out of their lived experience, questions they bring with them when they attend worship or carry with them long after they have ceased attending worship. One of the most famous sermons in Christian history is that preached by Arthur John Gossip in 1927 after the death of his wife. He took as a text the question from Jeremiah, "If you have run with the footmen and they have wearied you, then how can you contend with horses?" (12:5); and he shaped the sermon title as a question, "But When Life Tumbles in, What Then?"[4] Every so often a pastor will appeal to his congregation to submit questions for his sermon preparation. Years ago I secured a book of such sermons by famous preacher and pastor Lloyd John Ogilvie entitled *Ask Him Anything* with the subtitle *God Can Handle Your Hardest Questions.*[5] Then pastor of First Presbyterian Church of Hollywood and later Chaplain of the United States Senate, he used these questions as titles for twenty sermons, including:

- How Can God Know and Care about Me?

- Is It a Sin to Doubt?

- Why Are Some Christians So Dull?

- How Can I Forgive and Forget?

It is very difficult for the listener to avoid the seemingly automatic and perhaps momentary search for an answer to a question posed

---

[4] Clyde Fant and William Pinson, *20 Centuries of Great Preaching*, Volume VIII., (Waco, TX: Word, 1971), pp 232ff)

[5] (Waco, Texas: Word, 1981)

by a speaker. Every preacher—indeed, every public speaker—needs to know this and to take full advantage of the unique rhetorical power of the question.

Questions can be used as:

- Text, as when T J Pancake, AoP'10, preached his sermon "Letting Jesus Drive" from the famous text in Mark, chapter 8, "Who do people say that I am?...Who do you say that I am?" (*Beautiful*, 141-145); or

- Title, as when Gabriel Alemayehu AoP'11 preached on the Sabbath commandment at the 2011 National Festival with a sermon entitled "Got Rest?" (in *Waking*, 159-163); or

- Theme, as when Rashad Moore AoP'12, in his 2012 Festival sermon "Carriers of the Cross" mused while "sitting in that theater, I wrestled again with the question, 'What does it mean to be a follower of Christ and not just a fan?'" (*Uncommon*, 253-255); or

- Appeal, as in the testimonial sermon by Anne Marie Roderick, AoP'10, on the "The Lord's Prayer" (*Beautiful*, 157-161) where she concludes the sermon with this series of questions:

How would you name God's holiness?
How would you describe the immanence
and power of God?
What is your daily bread?
What forgiveness do you seek?

Have you forgiven everyone who has hurt
you?

How would you ask for God's protection?

Questions are useful as transition statements or concluding statements. Preachers often use a series of question to carry their appeal to the heart of the listener, and few elements of rhetoric can be as powerful as a succession of questions.

But perhaps the perfect use of questions came from the imagination of my then five-year-old grandson Samuel Wyatt Curson. He had accompanied me to a preaching service and heard me describe how some young ministers "play church" at home, using people and animals, even stuffed animals. After a stop for lunch during which more than one person ordered breakfast, he went right home, gathered his extensive collection of stuffed animals, arranged them into an assembly, and took his place standing on his bed. He started to preach with much animation and exertion, concluding his "sermon" with this wonderful appeal in the form of a question, "Now, do you want the Lord's green eggs and ham, or do you want the plain green eggs and ham?"

Sermon

In January of 2014, **Salvador Avila**, AoP'14, came from Southwestern Assembly of God University in Texas to preach at the National Festival of Young Preachers in Indianapolis. The preaching theme was "Questions of the Soul." Salvador took from the lists of assigned texts the famous question asked of Moses by God: "What is that in your hand?" Salvador used this question not only as the text and title of his sermon but also as his appeal to his listeners: "So I ask you today, what is that in your hand?" His sermon is both an example of how to use questions in preaching but also a challenge for us to make available to God the unique gifts God has given to us, even when it demands that we spend time in preparation. The sermon is published in *Questions* (13-16).

What is That in Your Hand?
Exodus 4:2

We all have something that represent us, symbolizing who we are, that represents our personality. A football can be the thing that represents a football player. When a person seen him with the football in his hand, they see his hard work, his dedication, his commitment, and his passion. For a musician, a piano or a guitar can be the very thing that represents his or her personality. When people see her playing piano or guitar, they see beyond the instrument to all of the hours of practice and sacrifices she has made. A carpenter has a hammer, a judge has a gavel, a lawyer has a briefcase, and a boxer has gloves.

We all have something that represents us. Moses had a staff that represented his identity as a shepherd. It symbolized his income because wealth was tied to livestock. It symbolized his influence as it was used to pull or push his sheep. The staff was what Moses knew best. The staff was all Moses had. Yet God turned that staff into the source of miracles and deliverance. This tells us that God uses ordinary things to accomplish extraordinary purposes.

God asked Moses, "What is that in your hand? (Exodus 4:2) God was not ignorant but God wanted to let Moses know that God was going to use Moses talent to accomplish something supernatural. God wanted Moses to realize the potential of the talent God had placed in his hand. God did not ask Moses to use something he did not have. God asked him to use something he already had.

God uses what we have, not what we do not have. We must develop what we do have, so God can use it to its full potential. The more we work on what we do have, the more God can use it. So I ask you today: what is in your hand? What is your strongest talent, your strongest gift? What do you know how to do best? What represents your personality? What represents who you are? What symbolizes you as a person?

Each of us has different talents and gifts. Some of you are gifted singers. Others are gifted leaders. Many of us here this weekend are preachers. Preaching is the staff God has placed in our hands. God wants to use our preaching to accomplish the salvation of humanity.

Moses is a picture of Jesus in the Old Testament, because he delivered God's people out of Egypt and led them to the Promised Land. Jesus came to deliver his people out of spiritual captivity and to the promise land of heaven. Moses spent 40 years in the desert and Jesus spent 40 days in the desert. There is a lot of similarity between Moses and Jesus.

I speak to you today about an aspect of the gift that God has placed in your hand. It will help you be much more effective at using your preaching gift. In order for us and for God to use our gift to its full potential, we must go through a preparation process. Moses had to go through it, and Jesus himself went through it. Great athletes don't win their games but in their training. In the same way, a preacher does preach a great sermon when he comes to the pulpit. The great sermon is preached in the preparation.

Why am I saying this?

Before Moses was ready to deliver God's people from captivity, he had to go through Midian. Midian is a necessary place of preparation that every man and woman God must go through. There is no shortcut. We must go through Midian. Moses spent about one-third of his life in the desert land of Midian. This time is forgotten by most Bible readers. The firs third and final third of his life are so much more dramatic. Yet Midian is one of the most crucial places in Moses' life.

Many of us are spending our time in Midian right now. We may not realize it or understand what is happening in our lives. Maybe the Lord is taking us through Midian right now. God is preparing us for what is in store for us in the years to come. God is equipping us to accomplish the calling God has for our lives. The season of Midian is not an easy season, but it is rewarded by God. Midian is a place where God works in our character, where God works on our attitude, where God works in our inner values and traits. So when we preach, we humble ourselves before God and acknowledge that God is the One working through us.

If Moses hadn't gone through those 40 years in Midian, he could have easily exalted himself and become arrogant when the Israelites were on the other side of the Red Sea. Never before in history had a miracle of that magnitude been performed. But Moses had been through Midian. Moses had walked with God for many years. He had done his homework. He had consecrated his staff to the Lord. His character had been shaped by the Lord. But in order to do everything he did, Moses had to go through Midian.

When you are going through Midian, you don't seek opportunities; you seek God and God's will. God takes care of opening the right door of opportunity at the right time and the right place for you.

These years in Midian don't feel like the most enjoyable years. These years are hard. We feel left out sometimes. But these years are necessary in equipping every man and women of God. Moses' ministry would bear much fruit. But in order for that to happen, God had to develop Moses' root system. Before a tree gives fruit, its root system must be developed. This process is like being in Midian.

I don't know what I am preaching to this morning. But I know that someone here has been praying, "God use me. I want to do great things for your glory and for your kingdom. Here I am, Lord. Do what you want to do in my life."

You have been working hard. You have been praying hard. You have been studying hard. You have been reading hard. But you have not yet seen the results or the opportunities you wish you had. God is saying to you, "What is that in your hand? It needs a little more preparation. Your time is coming. I am still developing that staff in your hand. I am preparing you and your gifts for the ministry I have in mind for you."

The biblical principal for us today is this: Offer what is in your hand to God. Live a life consecrated to God. Set yourself apart with God each day. Listen to God. Be patient in the land of Midian. This is what Jesus did. Every day before the sun rose, Jesus went to a solitary place and prayed. Then every day he went to the mission field where he ministered to people and delivered them from bondage. So I offer you an invitation: as we go home from this festival make a personal habit of going to Midian each day where we as preachers can listen to God. Then we can share God's message with God's people and change the world for Jesus. That is what is in my hand, and I offer it up to God!

Every Good Sermon
Includes a Metaphor

Metaphors are figures of speech, and Jesus was the master of the metaphor:

- I am the good shepherd. (John 10:11)

- The gate is wide and the road is easy that leads to destruction. (Mathew 7:13)

- Let your light shine before others. (Matthew 5:16)

Hardly a page of any of the Gospel narratives is void of some use of the imagination to communicate the truth. Paul the Apostle described the Christian as one protected by the armor of God (Ephesians); John the Apostle called upon Christians to live in the light (1 John 2:7-11); Peter the Apostle reminded his readers that the devil is a roaring lion, seeking to devour them (1 Peter 5:8); and James the Apostle asserted: "The tongue is a fire" (James 3:6). I suspect all of them could trace their use of metaphors to the Lord Jesus himself!

Some preaching traditions—especially the African American—emphasize the use of picture language, and this gives their young men and women an advantage in developing sermons. In his memorable sermon on the National Mall in 1963, Martin Luther King, Jr. is justly famous for the repetition of the phrase "I have a dream." Especially evocative was this sentence: "One hundred years later the Negro lives on a lonely island of poverty in the midst of a vast ocean of prosperity." But equally powerful was the extended metaphor that dominated the first part of that sermon:

> In a sense we've come to our nation's capital to cash a check. When the architects of our Republic wrote the magnificent words of the Constitution and the Declaration of Independence, they were signing a promissory note to which every American was to fall heir. This note was a promise that all men—yes, black men as well as white men—would be guaranteed the unalienable rights of life, liberty, and the pursuit of happiness. It is obvious today that America has defaulted on this promissory note insofar as her citizens of color are concerned. Instead of honoring this sacred obligation, America has given the Negro people a bad check, a check which has come back marked "insufficient funds."[6]

Those young preachers who grow up listening to this kind of preaching, where language pictures are a natural and essential part of the homiletic tradition, are blessed indeed. Other young ministers come from more rationalistic or didactic environments and will need to be very intentional about metaphors, which is why

---

[6] Martin Luther King, Jr, "I Have A Dream." (www.archives.gov/press/exhibits/dream-speech.pdf) accessed March 9, 2015.

I have this focus on metaphors in this collection of nine marks of a good sermon. Many seasoned speakers value poetry and urge young preachers to read and write poetry. One of my mentors, Ken Chafin, actually took up poetry writing after his retirement and published a book of poems. He said more than once he wished he had reversed those callings: poetry first, then preaching; which prompts me to offer this list of simple ways to train the imagination to see, think, and speak metaphorically.

> • Read poetry and lots of it. Shakespeare is excellent and so is Emily Dickinson: "Because I could not stop for Death, he kindly stopped for me; the carriage held but just ourselves and Immortality." All music—sacred and secular—runs over with metaphors; and don't forget about the poetry of the Bible: "The Lord is my shepherd" (Psalm 23:1).

> • Use metaphors in daily speech. Recently, I described the work of the Academy of Preachers as providing "the on-ramp to the homiletic highway."

> • Mark the metaphors in the Bible; memorize these texts; use them in sermons, prayers, and other ministerial speech. Set a goal of using a metaphor in every prayer, every sermons, and every presentation. At first, this will seem strained and unnatural; you may even feel awkward. But usage will take you to a place of comfort and skill, and your people will notice and be thankful; as I was upon

reading and re-reading the powerful sermon by Peter Marshall, "Get Out of Step."[7]

Nikia Williams was a student at Southern Polytechnic State University in Georgia when he came in January of 2013 to preach at the National Festival of Young Preachers in Atlanta. His sermon exhibited excellent use of metaphors drawn from the building trades, all of which he brought together in these four sentences in the conclusion to the sermon:

> Paul evangelized the Corinthians and wrote this letter to encourage them to have an Extreme Makeover: Faith Edition. First, go through demolition and rid themselves of those things keeping them from holding a relationship with God. Second, review the blueprint of purpose, knowing that God has destined us for greatness. And third, build with our renewed faith and live in our destiny (*Gospel*, 77).

Training the mind to see with metaphors (and the voice to speak with metaphors) will pay rich dividends in memorable and useful language, and the gospel of our Lord deserves every verbal advantage at our disposal.

---

[7] *John Doe, Disciple: Sermons for the Young in Spirit*, edited by Catherine Marshall (New York: McGraw-Hill, 1963), pp 94-106.

Sermon

Kristina (Tina) Heise, AoP'12, is a Lutheran preacher, having just graduated from the Lutheran School of Theology in Chicago. She came to the Academy of Preachers through a preaching camp in 2011 in Atlanta with 10 other fellows from the (then named) Fund for Theological Education—now the Forum for Theological Exploration. Her sermon "Smoothing out the Map," preached in Louisville at the 2012 National Festival of Young Preachers, makes wonderful use of metaphors. I count at least 20 metaphors, beginning with the title and including this wonderful sentence: "Fear was the foot that pushed the accelerator." Here is the entire sermon, taken from the book *Uncommon* (248-252).

Smoothing Out the Map
Matthew 7:13-14

It is said that home is where the heart is. We all have some form of home, be it the house we share with our spouse and children, our parents' apartment where we spend the holidays, or perhaps the sanctity of student housing. No matter where we hang our hat, our home is the place where we store treasures and build memories.

The universal hope is that everyone has a safe place to call home. The unfortunate reality is that not too many blocks from virtually any doorstep there are pockets of our neighborhoods of poverty, violence, and despair.

One day a seminary student (whom I will name Nicole) was driving her car through such a pocket on her way home from a church supply store. It was a beautiful fall day; the sun shone and the birds chirped. A few blocks ahead she saw children breaking free from a school day of math tests and heavy books.

Driving slowly toward the red light, Nicole noticed as a group of student drifted from the school and closer to a group of teenage boys standing at the corner of the street. Suddenly, she saw the smallest child from the school stumble onto the sidewalk. She watched dumbfounded as two of the teenagers began kicking and beating the younger boy, who lay on the ground.

Nicole was frozen, her brain not functioning as the horror of what she was witnessing fell upon her like a cold wind before the first snow. She sat in silent stillness at that red light while cries of pain from the small child floated through her cracked window.

After a moment, the traffic light turned green, and Nicole stepped on the gas. Moving forward with the traffic, she watched in her rearview mirror as the older children continued to beat the one on the ground. She did not know what to do but to drive away.

Later that night, Nicole watched the evening news and learned that two young men had been arrested for beating a young boy to death outside of his school.

In the weeks and months to follow, Nicole carried on her soul the bruises of the fateful day. She found herself wondering what this event said about her ability to be a good Christian and her ability to protect all people. She was a seminary student, after all, training to become a pastor. Surely, if anyone should have the moral integrity to stop a car and help a boy in danger, it should have been her. When she voiced these concerns to her family, they reminded her that she had no way of knowing if it was safe enough for her to help. They told her it was possible the older students carried weapons, that she would have risked endangering herself by turning to help. They claimed her instincts protected her from harm.

The family rationalizations made sense; yet still something did not sit quite right with Nicole. She is seeking to be a leader on behalf of God's family. If stopping a car was not a reasonable option, what other choices were there? Would a true leader have called the police? Friends quickly reminded her that she was not the only one on the road. Others could have called for help. She was no more wrong than the rest of the masses that drove by while the boy lay bleeding on the sidewalk.

Despite such thinking, despite the lists of "what if" and "who could have known", Nicole now lives with knowing she turned her back on the narrow gate of her humanity. She chose flight instead of fight and, in the process, chose the wider gate to the road most traveled. A song by Linkin Park states, "when the paper's crumpled up it can't be perfect again." The day Nicole drove through the wide gate, the paper of a young boy's innocence was not only crumpled but actually slipped through a hole in the pocket of that community.

Standing on the mount in Galilee Christ warns us to stop at red-light moments and look for the road that is not always easy. Nicole lost in the moment of her fear, in the shock of violence. In the rush and confusion of that moment, fear was the foot that pushed the accelerator.

Most of us will never experience the shock that Nicole witnessed that day outside the school. But our fear of knowing which way to turn can haunt us in all sorts of moments in our lives. For some, it is the fear of knowing whether it is better to stay in a loveless marriage or file for divorce. For others, it is the fear of applying to the better school or taking the scholarship offered by another school. Others face the fear of choosing between the comfort of the bottle and the ambiguity of rehabilitations.

The choice between roads such as these is challenging and may feel as big as the off-ramp of the interstate. Daily we must choose between roads that are as near to us as the street corner: the roads labeled Daly Prayer Parkway, Honest Avenue, and Eat Healthy Boulevard. These streets seem unimportant and are often neglected when the snow truck comes, but the impact from tone of its potholes will damage the ride to our salvation just the same.

There are many roads; there are many ways. The confusing darkness of various situations may operate like night vision blocking the signs for the most righteous exit. The radio of our fear may play so loud that we miss hearing the directions from our GPS. For not only could our ability to choose the right road but also to even see the gate before us.

The masses at the mount also experienced their share of obstacles. These were Jewish people, struggling to find the balance between the law of their ancestors and the pressures of their lives. Jesus understood this conflict. His sermon to this gathering resembles the poetic style of wisdom literature. This literature blends ethical insight with awareness of the arrogance of folly and the ignorance of insolence. Polarizing in presentation, wisdom literature contrasted righteous and wicked behavior: "The wicked flee when no one pursues, but the righteous are as bold as a lion" (Proverbs 28.1). "Happy is the one who is never without fear, but one who is hardhearted will fall into calamity" (28:14).

Jesus echoes the polarity found in wisdom literature and shows that living a righteous life is a matter of choice. Jesus tells us we can choose the narrow gate that leads to righteousness, or we can choose the wide gate the leads to wickedness. We can choose to go to rehab and get help, or we can choose to uncork another bottle of wine. We can choose to call the police when we see a child being attacked or we can drive away and hope someone else will step in.

Christ challenges us to be bold as a lion in touch moments. In our fear we are inclined to point toward the easy road and away from our sense of integrity. Jesus understands how fear can serve as a tranquilizer to even the strongest of beasts.

As both God and human, Christ feels the shake of the pen as we sign divorce papers. Christ's fingers punch the calculator as we assess potential school budgets. Christ's stomach turns in time with ours from substance withdrawal. When we walk the fin line that borders the pit, when we travel down the road that is too easy, Christ remains with us, experiencing the bruises of our fear.

Nicole was paralyzed that day outside the school that she chose the road of the masses, the wide gate of driving away. She through her only option was to turn around or turn away. In that moment she missed the third option: picking up the phone and calling for help. Like, Nicole, any one of us could have overlooked that exit. Christ meets us on this road. If we let him he will take control of the wheel.

The grace of forgiveness was given to us when Christ came down from the mountain and climbed upon the cross. All that is asked of us is to confess our sins and ask for guidance. Our God is not a cruel oppressor who lacks understanding. Instead, God offers continual forgiveness. It is true: once the paper of our soul is crumpled, it can't be perfect again. We can never go back before that first wrinkle. But God never promised we would be perfect, merely forgiven. A paper crumpled can still be smoothed out to display directions into a new future. The same paper that once carried the history of our sin now show the steps needed to turn our can around and head for the narrow gate.

With this bless of love and forgiveness before, we now have a path of choice. We can remain in our fear, ruled by the "what-if" and "who-could-have-known" memories. We can look in the rearview mirror and mourn those choices that slipped through our grasp. Or, with the love and support of Christ at our back and in our hearts, we can choose to be bold as a lion, smoothing out the map to the road less traveled.

Every Good Sermon
Tells the Story of Jesus

Jesus is at the center of gospel preaching. His story and its meaning for us today is the central focus of the Christian testimony. This is why the New Testament begins with the gospel narratives, even though they were not the first writings to emerge from the Christian movement. They constitute the stories that circulated among those first believers throughout the Mediterranean world in the first century. Likewise, telling listeners of the birth, life, ministry, death, and resurrection of Jesus is the first duty of the gospel preacher.

Every year the Academy of Preachers selects a preaching theme. In 2015, it is "Heaven & Earth," and in 2014 it was "Tell Me A Story." With all of these themes comes a selection of preaching texts and among these are always texts from the life, death, and resurrection of Jesus. But the first year, and periodically thereafter, the theme is simply Jesus, and we direct the young preachers to take any text from the story of Jesus. Our first volume of printed sermons was entitled *A Beautiful Thing* taken from a sermon by Lucas Rice AoP'10, then a student at St. Vladimir's Orthodox Theological Seminary; he preached on the episode recorded by Matthew when a woman named Mary anointed the head of Jesus with expensive perfume just days before his crucifixion. While all sermons do well to invoke Jesus in some way, here we are reminded that regularly, some sermons must focus on Jesus: his person, his message, his significance, his encounter with specific people. This is the heart and soul of Christian preaching and has been so from the beginning.

Preaching that sidelines Jesus is not Christian preaching; it may be excellent speech or effective motivation, but when it fails to present some part of the Jesus story, it ceases to be gospel preaching. Yes, there may be some occasions when explicit references to Jesus might be omitted; as in some public and civic occasions or a funeral for a person of another faith. But week by week, in the parish preaching to a Christian congregation, Jesus takes center stage.

There are Christian preachers and theologians who contend that texts from the Hebrew Bible (the Old Testament) can, and should, be interpreted without reference to Jesus; they assert that this orientation to Jesus misconstrues the original and essential meaning of the text. Sermons that truly and powerfully engage the text, therefore, can be preached without appeal to Jesus. Some of this contention is well placed; certainly true and helpful teachings on the Hebrew Bible without mentioning Jesus can be presented to the edification of the assembly; I have been the beneficiary of many. There is much good news in the Hebrew Bible, to be sure. But gospel preaching in the Christian assembly is testimony to Jesus and interpretation of Jesus.

The prime examples of Christian preaching in the apostolic era are the sermons in the book of Acts, and every preacher would do well to use them as a pattern. They tell stories of Jesus; they connect Jesus to the Hebrew/Jewish tradition; they interpret Jesus as the fulfillment of both Hebrew and human hopes; they call people to respond to the invitation of Jesus to live fully and faithfully in the kingdom of God. Peter's great Pentecost sermon can be summarized thus: God sent Jesus; evil men killed Jesus; God raised Jesus from the dead. Believe this good news and receive the Holy Spirit of God.

There are many ways to incorporate Jesus into Christian preaching:

- Jesus can be the theme of the sermon, as when David Smith AoP'12 preached on Matthew 9:35-38 with a sermon entitled "Following Jesus into Ministry" in *Gospel* (11ff).

- Jesus can be used to illustrate the theme of the sermon, as when Shantell Hinton AoP'14 answered the biblical question "Am I My Brother's Keeper?" with reference to Jesus, in *Questions* (118ff).

- Jesus can be invoked and quoted in the sermon, as when Tyler Ward AoP'11 developed his message on keeping Sabbath with the response of Jesus to his critics as recorded in Mark 2, in *Waking* (218ff).

- Jesus can be the center of the appeal, as when Dennis Strack AoP'14 called us to be like Jesus in his sermon about hope in the midst of trial, in *Questions* (218ff).

In some cases a preacher is wise simply to tell an episode from the life of Jesus; we must not assume that our people know the basic events of the life of Jesus. The most powerful resource at the disposal of any preacher is simply the life and teaching of Jesus; his story consistently inspires admiration, devotion and imitation—and this is the aim of gospel preaching.

Sermon

Craig Robinson, Jr. AoP'14 was a student at Yale Divinity School when he came to preach at the 2014 National Festival of Young Preachers in Indianapolis. The preaching theme that year was "Questions of the Soul." Craig selected the poignant question of King David about his son, "Is it well with the young man Absalom?" from 2 Samuel 18:32. Into this retelling of an episode that happened 1,000 years before the birth of Christ, Craig inserts Jesus—as an illustration of how to love. This sermon is taken from the book *Questions* (201-205).

The Whole Story
2 Samuel 18:32

It was too early in the semester for all of this commotion. That was what I was thinking to myself as I sat in the Bass Library of Yale University, trying to do some homework. Now if this were finals week, I would have known what all the commotion in the library was, because at the beginning of finals week, Yale undergraduates do their traditional naked run through the library. It is always a raucous affair that distracts even the most studious amongst us. But like I said, it was too early; it was the beginning of May—May 2, 2011, to be exact.

For some, May 2 might not be that significant a date, and for the moment it was just another study day for me. With all the commotion outside, I was becoming convinced that there was a holiday I was missing.

I immediately consulted that all-knowing source of information, Facebook, to gain some context for what I was hearing outside the library. Then I got the news: Osama bin Laden was dead. The commotion I heard was not the jovial shenanigans of naked undergraduates. No, the noise outside the library was the din of victory.

I went outside and saw students running and yelling across the central campus, American flags in hand, screaming "U.S.A.! U.S.A.! U.S.A.!" "The president and the special operatives got Osama bin Laden." America's enemy was vanquished! The most hated man of recent American history, destroyed! The destroyer of thousands of lives in New York City and elsewhere in our nation was no more. And the students, some of whom might have lost loved ones, celebrated with reckless abandon.

Facebook became inundated with status updates. Reactions ranged from high commendation to President Obama on a job well done to indignation in the face of all of the violence. Sides were taken. Lines were drawn. Arguments ensued! Those who showed sympathy for the slain al Qaeda leader and his family were lambasted for being unpatriotic. Those who celebrated his death were labeled cold and heartless by the righteously indignant.

I really didn't know how to feel. On one hand, I was grateful that the world was relieved of one more dangerous person. On the other hand, though, I felt overwhelmed at how violence continued to beget more violence. "But Osama bin Laden was our enemy; this was justice, right?" I asked myself. Well, that was the story.

The young man, Absalom, was the enemy. He usurped the king's throne, violated the king's house, and exiled the king himself to a distant land. He was the enemy! He was arrogant. He was violent.

He was crafty. He was the enemy! He was a traitor to the realm. He was a horrible despot. He was a bad son. He was David's enemy

"Is the young man all right? Is the young man safe?" asked David.

Haven't you been following the story? Haven't you been listening to the news? This young man just tried to destroy you; who cares? He's your enemy. I know it's not what you want to hear, but … That was Absalom's story!

I recently saw a TED talk presented by famed Nigerian author Chimamanda Ngozi Adichie entitled "The Danger of a Single Story."[8] In that presentation she lamented the limited literary choices available to her in her youth. All of the books were written by white authors colored by white privilege, and there was only one story being told. The analogy was extended to other facets of life and the power of the storyteller to create or destroy life with a single story. A single story is dangerous, she said, because it does not consider the dynamism of the individual. A single story is dangerous because it does not give full perspective of who we are and who we can become. A single story robs the individual of authentic living.

Is there anybody here who has been the victim of a single, myopic, unimaginative story? Spun by someone who has no interest in who you are? No investment in your development? You can't be this or

---

[8] Adichie, Chiamamanda Ngozi. "The Danger of a Single Story," www.ted.com, accessed January 1, 2014. www.ted.com/talks/chimamanda_adichie_the_danger_of_a_single_story.html

that because you're gay. You're a woman. You're black. You're too privileged. You're too big. You're not educated enough.

For most of chapter 18 of 2 Samuel, the story that Joab and the rest of the loyal subjects of King David told was that the young man Absalom was the enemy and deserved to die! And then you get to verse 32. Here, another story emerges. Absalom is not just an enemy of the state. No, here he is David's beloved son. Is the young man Absalom all right? I told my captains, I told my soldiers, deal gently with him. Is he all right? I thought I had made myself clear. Please tell me Absalom is all right!

You know, love is many things. It is in Paul's words: patient, kind, humble. The writer of John's letter says that love is the very essence of God: "God is love" (I John 4:8). Love is many things, and love can also do many things. Love can comfort. It can heal a broken heart. It can soothe a hurting soul. And it can make things complicated. Ask anybody who has been in love. They will tell you just how complicated love can make things.

The things we do for love. You did what?! But I love him. You went where?! But I love her. You spent how much on dinner?! But I'm in love …

For the parents in the room with crazy-acting kids, love will certainly keep you from doing what your right mind tells you to do. My mother, God love her, would quickly remind me that she brought me in this world and could easily take me out. Thank God for love manifested in a mother's mercy!

Love complicates things. Love is powerfully disorienting. It does not allow for a single story to prevail. Love manages to look past the faults that justice would illumine. Love asks what happened and how can we make things better? Loves looks for what can be redeemed. Love does not allow simple, uncritical black or white answers to be the end of the matter. Love pricks the soul and sometimes makes us ask crazy questions like the one David asked, "Is the young man Absalom all right?"

This question tells another story. It tells a whole story. It transforms Absalom from an enemy to be eliminated or a cancer to be cursed into a child of the king who, above all else, needed to be cared for, understood, even reconciled.

Howard Thurman in his book *Disciplines of the Spirit*[9] says in the chapter on "Reconciliation" that "the concern for reconciliation finds its expression in the simple human desire to understand others and to be understood by others….Every man (and woman) wants to be cared for, to be sustained by the assurance that he shares in the watchful and thoughtful attention of others" (105). The need to be cared for is essential to the furtherance and maintenance of life.

I don't know if what Thurman is suggesting is a perfect solution. I know plenty of skeptical people who would bristle at the notion of understanding one's enemy or showing care and concern for those who mean us harm. But in the face of more violence and destruction of land and life, Thurman's suggestion is as good a place as any to start.

Let's face facts: We all have some enemies. There are people and systems that mean to do us harm. But shall we fight evil with evil? Or shall we cure evil with good? Will we, the followers of Jesus

---

[9] Howard Washington Thurman. *Disciplines of the Spirit* (Richmond, IN: Friends United Press, 1963).

Christ, give reconciliation a try? When our enemies are on our track, will we endeavor to find out the whole story? Will we quit our anger long enough to give our enemy the space for grace that might reveal their true feelings, needs, and desires? Will we take the time to get the whole story?

It is not easy, and that is why Thurman called reconciliation a spiritual discipline, one that must be attempted over and over again until change comes.

David's question is one we as Christians should take special note to remember. In his unfailing love for his son, he reminds us that even the worst of people in our mind is not beyond the reach of love and reconciliation.

This is also the testimony of David's greater son, Jesus Christ, our Lord, whose ministry of reconciling a dying world, enemies of God, began by caring acts and the refusal to reduce any one of God's children to a single, unimaginative story: whether it was a woman at the well with a story of five partners and no husband, to a woman with an issue of blood, to a blind man whose condition plagued him from birth; or Levi, the tax collector, or Zaccheus. Not one was beyond God's loving reach, even if their stories labeled them unworthy of such attention.

If we are going to heal this world of hatred and anger and violence, even our enemies must know that they are not beyond the reach of God's love.

As I returned to my seat and refreshed my Facebook page, the battles continued to rage; expressions of joy and lament, celebration and consternation. And I did not know what to do.

Then I began to think more about all the loss, on both sides of the conflict, since that fateful day in 2001. I thought about the thousands of lives affected by the twin towers' collapse. I thought about all of the justifiably angry Afghan people who have been victims of America and other world powers' exploitation of their homeland. I thought about Osama bin Laden's family.

And in my mind I did what my Christian conscience called me to do. I prayed—for everybody. I prayed for the U.S.A. and I prayed for Afghanistan. I prayed for President Obama and I prayed for the repose of Osama bin Laden's soul.

Because I understood; I understood the story. I understood it was complicated. And I understood what Jesus meant when he said, "Love your enemies."

Every Good Sermon
Issues a Clear Call to Action

The fundamental and repeatable message of Jesus was some version of this: "The rule of God is near. Repent and believe this good news" (Mark 1:15, et. al). In other words, Jesus declared the good news, then called for a response. Jesus made an appeal for action. "Repent and be baptized" is the way Peter responded when asked by his hearers, "What shall we do?" (Acts 2:38). Both of these are classic appeals to people to do something in response to what they have heard. Such appeals have been, from the beginning of the Christian movement, a basic element of the gospel sermon.

The call to action can be:

- Trust God

- Confess your sins

- Welcome the stranger

- Pray without ceasing

- Search the Scriptures

- Take hold of eternal life

- Be still and know that I am God

These are just a few of the many invitations that can punctuate or conclude a good gospel sermon. Tyler Best, AoP'12, illustrates this perfectly in his sermon "No More Bubbles!" preached at the 2013 National Festival of Young Preachers in Atlanta when he was a sophomore at the University of Evansville. Note also the excellent use of a question to conclude a sermon with a strong appeal.

> This morning, throughout the remainder of the festival, and even as you return to your home ministry, I pray that you will join me in praying for unity like we have never seen it before. I pray for a sense of intentional unity among the body of Christ in your city. I pray for a sense of unity that is noticeable by all people, to the glory of God. Our Father in heaven wants his people not just tolerant of one another; God doesn't just want us slightly acquainted; instead, God calls for a close family working together for the kingdom. Our savior died to make it possible. Out of the ashes of hostility and hate between the Jews and Gentiles, the Holy Spirit brought about true beauty. Can we seek that same beauty in our own Christian community today? (*Gospel*, 81)

The presence of a strong and clear call does not turn the gospel preacher into a salesman, although many preachers have tended in this direction. Much criticism has been properly directed toward those who use emotion to manipulate listeners into actions (including those that relate to money!) that are unwise, inappropriate, and disconnected to the gospel. But the presence of an altar call or public invitation does not necessarily distort the gospel call. In fact, such tactics have been instrumental in mobilizing millions of people to faithful service in the kingdom of God. War hero Louis Zamperini witnesses to just such an experience, as narrated in the book *Unbroken: A World War II Story of Survival, Resilience, and Redemption.*[10]

One of my favorite sermonic appeals, though, it is one described in Neil Diamond's ballad "Brother Love's Traveling Salvation Show."

> Now brothers, you got yourself two good hands.
> And when your brother is troubled
> You got to reach out your one hand for him,
> `cause that's what it's there for.
>
> And when your heart is troubled
> You got to reach out the other hand,
> reach it out to the man up there,
> `cause that's what he's there for.

Sermonic appeals do not have to be so forceful or overt. Professor Robert Reid of the University of Dubuque unveils for us what he calls the four "voices" of preaching. He analyzed American sermons and grouped them into four types based on the response expected by the preacher. The four responses are:

- "Yes, that is what I believe!"

- "Lord, let that happen to me!"

- "Whoa, what am I going to do with that?"

---

[10] Laura Hillenbrand (New York: Random House, 2010)

<ul>
<li>"I think we need to talk some more."</li>
</ul>

These four types of responses to sermons help people understand their preacher and also help preachers understand their own intentions and expectations; I know it was an eye-opener for me, and not just about other preachers. These types or "voices" illustrate the full range of sermon responses, from the subtle to the sturdy, from the overt to the implied. But each shares this one thing: the expectation of response to what has been preached. All have a distinctive element of provocation to action, even if that "action" is contemplation or conversation.

Abraham Lincoln is reputed to have complained upon leaving church one Sunday: "He never tells us what to do" (thus illustrating, perhaps, a preacher with the sage voice). I, too, have departed many a sanctuary unsure of what the preacher was calling me to do. Personally, I prefer the appeal that is strong, clear, and direct. "Lay aside the sin that clings so closely," Hebrews urges us, "and let us run with perseverance the race that is set before us" (Hebrews 12:1). There is a clear, sturdy call to action—using a powerful metaphor! Let every preacher be clear as to what he wants the people to do—or else be silent!

Sermon

The soft appeal is wonderfully employed by **Scott Woods**, AoP'14, in his sermon "Who do you Say That I Am?" He preached at the 2014 National Festival of Young Preachers in Indianapolis, not far from his school in southern Indiana, St. Meinrad Seminary. This sermon, taken from the book *Questions* (262-265) calls upon all of us to make the good confession about Jesus Christ as Lord and Savior and does so in a most appealing way.

Who Do You Say That I Am?
Matthew 16:13-20

Typing "who is Jesus?" into Google yields 533 million results in a mere 25/100 of a second. For those of us who glory in the name Christian, it is also an absolutely crucial one. This question for the ages finds its way onto the covers of popular mainstream magazines and is the premise of cable television specials. The search is undoubtedly on for the man from Nazareth behind the name above all names, as it has been for 2,000 years.

You and I rightfully turn to the Gospels as we strive to determine who Jesus is. "Who is Jesus?" is the central question that Matthew, Mark, Luke, and John were seeking to answer from start to finish. Yet even the Gospel writers offer different explanations! Matthew holds no punches. He identifies Jesus as the son of David and Abraham right from the get-go. He then meticulously situates Jesus 42 generations from our father in faith so that it's clear that Jesus is the promised one whom the prophets foretold. Mark paints a portrait of a hidden messiah who is the suffering servant of the

Lord. Luke shows us that Jesus is the universal savior whose compassion knows no bounds. Then there is John, with his high Christology, revealing a Jesus who is the eternal word made flesh.

So, who is Jesus? He is a man on a mission. He travels the countryside, roaming from village to village, ministering to multitudes with his troupe of lackluster fishermen who really aren't sure what they're doing or why they're following him.

Who is Jesus? He is a healer of ills. His path intersects with those who are possessed. The demons know who he is: the holy one of God who has come to destroy the tormentors of God's people and reclaim them as his own. Paralytics, crying out to him, are ordered to take up their mats and go on their way. He opens the eyes of the blind who then see not only a miracle worker but the human face of God standing before them. He heals lepers of their physical sores as well as the disease of isolation they have endured for years.

Who is Jesus? He is a teacher par excellence. He scales Tabor's heights and speaks as the new Moses, declaring the weak and the oppressed to be blessed. He is an artist of words who employs the similes of salt and light to explain the divinely given mission of his followers. He detests anger and places a premium on such impossible tasks as loving one's enemies. Like any good teacher, he sounds a little crazy, he thinks outside the box, and he opens the eyes of his students so they might see in a new way. He leaves people asking, "Who is this? Who is this who speaks with such authority?" (paraphrased from Mark 4:41 and Matthew 7:29).

Brothers and sisters, the sacred scriptures surely reveal that Jesus is indeed Emmanuel, the Son of God born of Mary, the fulfillment of ancient prophecies whom magi from the east journeyed to adore. He is the Lamb of God whom John announced and reluctantly baptized. He is the master who walked along the Sea of Galilee and summoned those fishermen to cast their nets into a sea teeming with floundering men and women instead of fish. He is the teacher who speaks with authority, and yes, he is the divine physician who expels demons, heals hemorrhaging women, and raises Lazarus from the dead. It is true; all of it is true. The question that Jesus asks Simon and us, however, is not "who does scripture say I am?" or "who does the church say I am?" but "who do *you* say that I am?" (Matthew 16:15)

Jesus doesn't let Simon hide behind the stock answers, and neither can we. Simon's is a confession of faith, pure and simple. It's not a theological treatise, though it has theological ramifications for us. No, Simon's confession rises up from deep within his heart. It's the result of a personal, life-changing encounter with the Christ. It is for us as well.

Jesus turns toward us, as he did Simon, gazing directly into our eyes, penetrating our very souls, asking, "Who do you say that I am?" Formed by scripture and tradition, we may make a confession similar to Simon's. We may claim Jesus as the Messiah, the son of the living God, but what does that mean—not theologically, but personally? Do we know about Jesus or do we know Jesus?

So what that he is Emmanuel, if we are unaware of his presence within and among us? So what that he is the master, if we refuse to submit our human will to the divine will? So what that he speaks with authority, if we've written him off and tuned him out because what he says is too inconvenient or difficult to do? So what that he is the divine physician, if we don't know that we're sick, or worse yet, refuse to swallow the antibiotic of God's mercy, the medicine that heals the devastating infection of sin that plagues us and threatens to entirely consume us? So what, brothers and sisters, that Jesus is all these things, if we don't know him and who he is for us, and if our response doesn't emerge from deep within us as it did from Simon?

Matthew's version of this exchange between Jesus and Simon, an event common to the gospels of Matthew, Mark and John, is unique because Matthew gives us the "so what." Simon got Jesus right, though he'll still get him wrong. But his response changes him. Simon is no more; he's Peter now. He is the rock on which the church shall rise and flourish to the glory of God. Simon received a new identity when he came to understand who Jesus is for him and what claim Christ makes on his life.

Relationship with the son of the living God changed Simon. It changes us, too. Simon, that occasionally successful fisherman who cast his nets into the Sea of Galilee, is now Peter, the fisherman of people. The boat he navigates through the treacherous waters of the world is the church built firmly upon his faith. His relationship with the Christ of God freed him from himself, his old self, from the missteps of the past and the guilt and shame that accompany them. Remember, though, we're talking about Peter. We know the rest of the story; he wasn't made perfect by his declaration of faith in Jesus. But, brothers and sisters, Peter's confession was not about perfection, and neither is ours!

Yes, Peter struggled with sin. He got discipleship wrong from time to time. This is the man who rebuked the Messiah shortly after confessing his belief in him. He even denied the son of the living God three times! Despite his confession of faith, Peter still needed the Christ to suffer, die, and rise for him in Jerusalem, and his faith slowly but surely freed him from sin's despair and opened his heart to that tremendous gift of divine mercy and the hope of a new beginning. It is for us as well!

Our confession must not be confused with perfection. We who answer the Lord's question, "Who do you say I am?" will not be made perfect, nor will we be suddenly preserved from sin. But answering that question as did Simon will surely change us. It will shape the way we live our lives. Confessing Jesus as Lord of our lives will free us for mission, Christ's mission. We will leave behind our nets crafted to grab fame, fortune, and success. We will cast aside our fretting over who we, our family, our friends, and the culture say we should be because we know who we truly are: beloved children of God. As we have been called, healed, and taught, so will the Lord who has freed us from our former way of life call, heal, and teach through us.

Confessing Jesus as Lord will make our arms and hands his own as he reaches out, through us, to alleviate the misery of the poor and the outcast. Confessing Jesus as Lord will make our legs and feet his own as he stands up, through us, to the demons of selfishness and injustice that possess God's people still. Confessing Jesus as Lord will make our voice his own as the eternal word continues to speak, through us—a word of love instead of hate, a word of forgiveness instead of bitterness, and a word of peace instead of strife.

Brothers and sisters, our confession of faith in Christ Jesus is not about titles and words. It's about an encounter and a relationship with the son of the living God, by which we are changed for the better. Our confession will not make us perfect, but it will change us. It will free us. It will renew us. It will make us signs of his presence in the world. Like Peter, we, too will rebuke the outrageousness of the gospel at times. We will deny our relationship with Jesus when we mistreat our brothers and sisters in whom he dwells. Nonetheless, our confession will give us a share in Jesus' mission for which he lived and died. Our confession will be for us, as it was for Peter, the first step on a long journey of faith that will guide us through this life and lead us over the threshold of death to life everlasting with Jesus our Lord.

Every Good Sermon
Displays the Passion of the Preacher

Not all sermons need a double dose of urgency, but every sermon needs to be full of conviction—not intensity, necessarily (and many confuse these two features of public speech)—but conviction: the feeling that the speaker is giving voice to what he really believes, to what is true and useful and important, to what will make a difference in life and death.

Johnny Cash learned this lesson the first time he auditioned at Sun Studio in Memphis, Tennessee (according to the 2005 movie *Walk the Line*). Cash (played by Joaquin Phoenix) aspired to be a gospel singer; so he and two fellow musicians prepared a bland version of a Jimmy Davis song popular in that day. When they completed their studio performance, Sam Phillips (played by Dallas Roberts) looked him in the eyes and said, "Is that all you got?"

Johnny did not know what to say, but Phillips did; and what he said about singing is doubly true of preaching. Here is that scene, and I take the liberty to transpose Phillips' references to singing into the language of preaching:

> Suppose you was hit by a truck, and you was lying
> out in that gutter dying, and you had time to

preach one sermon. One sermon people would remember before you're dirt. One sermon that would let God know what you felt about your time here on earth, one sermon that would sum you up. You're telling me that's the sermon you'd preach …? Or would you preach something different, something real, something you felt? I'm telling you right now, that's the kind of sermon people want to hear; that's the kind of sermon that truly saves people.

It was, according to the movie, a turning point in the career of Johnny Cash, and it can be a turning point in your ministry. It is this element of passion, conviction, and deep soul that sets apart the good gospel preacher from the hundreds of men and women who stand in the pulpit and repeat just what everybody else is saying and has said for hundreds of years.

The truly powerful preaching in the Bible (and in church history) exhibit just what Phillips said to Cash that day in Memphis, Tennessee. It was an emotional moment when Moses declared to the people: "Today I set before you life and death." The perennial popularity of the Psalms lies primarily with the emotional way they give voice to the highs and lows of life, from "Bless the Lord, O my soul" (103:1) to "How long, O Lord?" (35:17) Jeremiah was known as the weeping prophet, and Amos was intense in his demand that "justice roll down like waters" (5:24). Jesus quoted Isaiah when he turned over the tables, saying, "My house is a house of prayer for all people." Peter must have been as full of emotion as he was of the Spirit when he stood on Pentecost to declare, "You killed Jesus but God raised him from the dead" (paraphrased from Acts 2:22-32). And even today we cannot read the powerful words of Paul the apostle without absorbing the emotion: "Who can separate us from the love of God? ... I am persuaded that neither life or death, nor angels nor rulers, nor things present nor things to come, nor powers, nor height nor depth, nor anything else in all creation will be able to separate us from the love of God in Christ Jesus our Lord" (Romans 8:38-39).

Of course, with passion, as much as any other of these nine marks of a good sermon, how something is said is secondary to what is said. If there is no substance, so seriousness, no truth, no relevance, no genuine gospel, then all the enthusiasm, emotion, and passion available to the human is of little good; it is like the fog that the sun drives away or the meringue that adorns a pie but does not nourish the body or assuage the hunger. Didn't Shakespeare describe something as "full of sound and fury but signifying nothing"? He could have been talking about some preaching! I certainly have heard many sermons that fell into that category (and I myself have preached a few).

Passion does not require volume or length or anger or a demand that people think or live in a certain way. This is important to note, for some people, preachers and parishioners alike, equate passion with perspiration—if the preacher is not constantly reaching for the handkerchief to mop his brow, he has not sufficiently put his soul into the sermon, or if she has not raised her voice high enough or marched around the platform far enough. These may be signs of passion, but not necessarily. Quiet intensity and personal testimony can be as full of passion as raucous rambling and dramatic story. Nevertheless, passion does require a level of enthusiasm and a wellspring of energy—enough to convey to the congregation that the preacher is speaking from the heart as well as the head.

Passion is an emotion, and preaching that suppresses the emotional element of speaking or hearing is not doing justice to the gospel ministry. Some traditions seek to suppress emotion: in preaching, in worship, and in religion in general. But this is a mistake. Nothing of importance ever happened without a level of enthusiasm, a good deacon used to say to me; and I believe it.

Good preaching—as the rhetoricians stated long ago—has an appeal to the reason, the will, and the emotions, and the good preacher will leave none of these gospel stones in her purse when she stands to preach.

Sermon

Wallis C. Baxter III AoP'11 was a student at Howard University when he came to preach at the 2011 National Festival of Young Preachers in Louisville, Kentucky. The preaching theme was "The Ten Commandments," and Wallis took as his text the Transfiguration narrative recorded in Luke 9:28-36. His sermon title is "A Gathering of Old Men," taken from a book title whose approach to history bears a striking resemblance to that of Luke the evangelist. The sermon as originally preached can be found in *Waking* (294-298).

A Gathering of Old Men
Luke 9:28-36

African American novelist Ernest Gaines penned a novel in 1983 entitled *A Gathering of Old Men.*[11] This novel is a mystery or detective novel. It tells parts of a narrative that is only fully understood after each character's portion of the story has been witnessed.

The novel is centered in the events comprising the strange and mysterious death of Mr. Beau Boutan. Can you picture it? Law officers arrested one individual already and charged him with murder, yet there are still some questions as to exactly what happened. The sheriff decides to interrogate those who are close to, or conspiring with, the convicted party. These old men who are interviewed strangely accept individual responsibility for the murder. In accepting responsibility for the murder of Beau Boutan,

---

[11] New York: Knopf, 1983

these old men affirm not only their capacity to speak but also their ability to act. The main action of the narrative is limited to a single day's events. However, the various memories voiced by the community enable the reader to experience the past as well. Through several audible encounters, the present is merged with the past.

This is the task before Gaines: how do we bridge the gap between current mystery and former activity? In other words, in what way can we show how today's events are in connection with and are a direct result of no0so-current history?

I contend that the evangelist Luke has painted a similar picture for us here today. The fact of the matter is that our text presents us with a *mysterium tremendum* a grand mystery.

Let us examine this divine mystery.

Any time the Bible depicts the presence of God, there arises a certain sense of mystery and elusiveness. As we look here in the ninth chapter of Luke, we pause and ask ourselves, "Is this really happening?" Like the disciples in this Transfiguration account, we must find some meaning in this extraordinary turn of events.

The disciples had watched Jesus pray on several occasions, but Luke is careful to note the exclusiveness of this particular prayer meeting. This transfiguration occurs eight days after a profound proclamation of Jesus: Jesus said if they would follow him they would indeed enter into the kingdom of God.

This eighth day phenomenon bears some significance to this Lukan account. In the book of Leviticus if you wanted to be clean from sin you had to bring some turtledoves on the eighth day. If somebody in your life did something wrong you would bring your first-born lamb or cold to the priest on the eighth day. John the Baptist was circumcised and received his name on the eighth day. Here eight days later, Jesus goes to the mountain to pray. According to the Jesus calendar, Jesus actually died on a Friday but got up on the eight day. Therefore a Christian reader of Luke's gospel must arrive at verse 29 with a certain sense of anticipation for what will happen n the eighth day. The entire scenario is full of divine mystery.

Jesus is transfigured. He is illuminated as the disciples look on seemingly from afar, for they see his glory. Then, suddenly, Jesus is no longer alone. In an instant Luke, like Gaines, merges the past and the present in a unique manner. Moses and Elijah are seen with Jesus discussing Jesus' own exodus. This gathering of old men is critical to understanding the significance of this obscure story. Yes, we see remnants of the Old Testament in the New Testament. But Luke is doing something quite unique. It is true that many sayings from the OT are represented in the NT. It is true that Jesus even restates the Torah as well as the prophets. It is true also that many of the customs and traditions practiced in the OT are found in the NT. Yet, Luke in a very craft way goes even further. He brings these two well known OT figures. Luke forces the reader to look at the present situation while not forgetting, omitting, or letting go of the past.

First, we see Moses. He is that great leader of the Israelites who was called by God to guide the Children of Israel to the Promised Land. The giving of the law of Mount Sinai enshrined the historical legacy of Moses. Along with Moses, we see Elijah, who represents the prophets. Elijah is the prophet's prophet. John the Baptist was the one to go before the Messiah in the spirit and power of Elijah. Some even considered Jesus to be Elijah. Moses and Elijah were both revered. They appeared, like Jesus, in glory. Here, again, a convergence of the old and new. These two old men appear in Glory. They appear to be of likeness to Jesus.

This definitive meeting helps us understand the assignment for the rest of Jesus' life. We, also, have had, are having, or will have a definitive meeting with the Lord at a particular time in our lives. It often happens when you least expect it. But an encounter with the true and living God always established something, always evokes something, always enlighten us in some way. When we leave that definitive meeting, we come out with our marching orders; we know what we are to do.

When you attend his meeting, something will be changed.

- If you are lost, you will come out with a new direction.

- If you are lonely, you will come out with renewed fellowship.

- If you are sick, you will come out with a remedy for your ailment.

- If you are depressed, you will come out inspired.

- If you are oppressed, you will come out liberated.

In this way Luke presents Jesus as receiving his distinct mission. The old man Moses is there to validate Jesus as keeper and proclaimer of God's law, and the old man Elijah is there to authenticate Jesus as rightful heir to the prophets. By their reaffirming Jesus' death or exodus, we can draw the conclusion that they have said their part. So now let us turn our attention to the third old man, Jesus. Yes, Jesus is young, but if we look at his pre-existence Jesus, is, in fact, old as well.

Luke presents Jesus who is the result of a long tradition. Jesus is, in fact, an old soul. He is not just the fulfillment of the Law; he is the Law. He is not only the fulfillment of the prophecy, he is the origin of prophecy. Jesus is the Son of God. Now we come to a picture of Jesus as his chosen Son with a distinct mission. We also have a distinct mission. We have been called to do one thing: to share Christ with all we encounter.

Ernest Gaines portrays a society that will be altered by the deaths of its old men. He presents an allegory about the passion of the old and the birth of the new. The new generation has the task of keeping alive the significance and relevance of the old. Moses is dead. Elijah is gone. Moses died and was buried allowing hope to abide with God's children Elijah is taken up to allow him to be a future of faith and hope. Jesus was crucified, buried, and taken up as the hope for all nations and generations.

Yes, Jesus is left all alone after the Transfiguration. But the good news is that he is confirmed. He is established. Jesus is Lord. Enemies may chastise; haters may criticize, but Jesus is Lord. Detractors may distract, disciples may doubt, but Jesus is Lord. Counselors may misguide, professors may not inspire, but Jesus is Lord.

When they talk about you, when they mistreat you, when they call you everything but a child of God, Jesus is Lord. If the walls close in, if the ceiling begins to lower, if the floor gives way, Jesus is Lord. No matter the situation, no matter the circumstance, no matter now dark and dim it seems, Jesus is Lord.

The disciples realized that Jesus was Lord. The text declares they told no one. I don't know about you, but when I think of the goodness of Jesus, and all that he's done for me, I can't help it: I have to run and tell somebody that Jesus is Lord.

Because he is Lord, I have some more good news: He lives.

Because he lives, I can sing, because he lives, I can should.

Because he lives, I can give God praise.

Fire in My Bones

This sermon was preached on Saturday, January 8, 2011, in the Cathedral of the Assumption in Louisville, Kentucky. It was the concluding sermon in the 2011 National Festival of Young Preachers. Our theme that year was "The Ten Commandments," but I (as well as the preacher who preceded me, on Friday night—Dr. Robert Smith) took Jeremiah 1:7-11 as my text. I print the sermon here because it illustrates my use of all nine marks discussed in this book. I have taken the liberty to note in the margins these nine homiletic elements in the hope that young preachers might be intentional in building these nine marks into your sermon preparation. This sermon is also published in *Waking* (425-430).

Story

A forest fire rages out of control in California. We see pictures of firefighters. Some swing picks. Some drive trucks. Some stare in despair across the ravished hills and ravines. Helicopters rescue stranded people and fire planes drop tons of retardant. People sob as they watch their homes go up in flames. It is always sad.

Some days later an announcement: authorities in California have identified the origin of the recent wildfire. Four college students were camping but failed to properly extinguish a fire. They show us a picture of the campsite, then the faces of four people. I

99

am always impressed that, in the midst of so many square miles of scorched earth, anybody could discover when and where it all started.

I feel the same way when I read the preaching of Jeremiah. It is the most chaotic collection of material in the Bible. Like a wildfire, it rages, without order: in the temple, from a cistern, at the city gate, and from the court of the guard. Scholars debate the chronology of his life. Square in the middle of this muddled collection we call the prophecy of Jeremiah, the preacher himself confesses, "There is within me something like a burning fire, shut up in my bones. I am weary from holding it in and I cannot" (20:9).

Who lit this wildfire of weal and woe? And when? And how?

When Jeremiah looks back on his life, when he pens his memoirs, when he puts down on paper the events and episodes of his life, he answers this question. He adds to his chronicle of seasoned prophecy an episode from his youth: a prologue, the preacher called it last night.

Let us look to this prologue for clues to the prophetic fire: where it started and when and how. It will help you, young preachers, realize that what is happening to you, even this day, will shape your life. God is lighting a fire in you that you cannot quench or control.

Jeremiah remembers what God said to him as a boy. He shares with us a teenage memory: "Before you were born, I selected you," the Lord said to Jeremiah early in his life. "I anointed you a preacher to the nations" (1:5). Not just to your congregation, not just to your denomination, not just to the Christian community, but to the world, to the nations, to the human community. The message you have of justice and judgment, of salvation and redemption is something needed by the whole world. The message you have of truth, peace, beauty, and hope is a word the whole world needs to hear.

In these matters Jeremiah is like Jesus. Not just that Jesus also received his call early in life. Not just that Jesus also suffered misunderstanding, torture, and rejection. For both Jesus and Jeremiah, the call was not confined to the synagogue or the temple, to the first century or the Syrian coast. Jesus and Jeremiah had a word for the world, his world and our world, my world and your world.

But when this word of anointing, of vocation, of calling came to Jeremiah, he

101

resisted. He pushed back. Jeremiah protested, "I am too young" (1:6).

Some of you are nervous about your age. And some of your elders want to keep you in your place. "These young people must wait their turn," one older preacher said to me. You must honor your elders, finish your degree, receive their approval, accept their timetable. Right? Except that:

Mother Teresa began her mission in India at age 18.

Andrew Gillum was elected a city commissioner in Tallahassee at age 23.

Lebron James signed an NBA contract at age 19.

Mark Zuckerberg launched Facebook at age 20.

Jackie Evancho is singing like an opera star at age 10.

Perhaps God read a similar list to Jeremiah. No doubt God then added that most often repeated command in the Bible: "Do not be afraid." That is the word of God to you today: Do not be afraid!

Do not be afraid of your youth.

Yes, you lack degrees, and experience, and wisdom, and opportunity. Yes, I know that. But you have what this sixty-year-old preacher doesn't have: energy, vision, passion, surrender, sacrifice, a lifetime of consecration ahead of you. The history of spiritual renewal and moral revival is largely the story of young people.

Preachers my age are focused on retirement, the stock market, the cost of health insurance, and how to keep peace in the church. The fire is burning low. In many of my colleagues, it is nothing but embers. What kind of fire can we light? You think we can be the change you want to see? We are singing out of hymnals, for God's sake!

God says to you today: Do not be afraid. Chisel that above the doorway of your house. Set that to music and make it your ring tone. If you sign up for God's Twitter account, this is what you will hear: Do not be afraid. 16 characters. God does not need all 144 characters allotted. God needs just 16. DO NOT BE AFRAID.

Do not fear your age.

And do not be afraid of your own voice.

103

Jeremiah said, "I do not know how to speak. My speech is halting, ignorant, stammering, confused, provincial, dull, empty, flat, boring. Dear God, I cannot speak to hold the attention of my mother, let alone a congregation of your people." Perhaps Jeremiah sought another way to fulfill God's purpose in his life.

Go see the movie *The King's Speech.* Be warned. There is no violence. No sex. No special effects. No fast cars or bloody faces. But it is a true story of a man whose vocation in life required him to speak in public. The movie will remind you of the power of public speech. It will inspire you to overcome any barriers to effective communication.

Some of you are tempted to abandon the voice. You say to yourself, we live in the digital age, the era of images. Movies are the wave of the future. "A picture is worth a thousand words," you quote and think the matter is settled.

Not so fast.

The most powerful thing in the world is the human voice. When I leave here I will drive an hour east to my home, there to be greeted by my grandson, who will spread his arms and say some version of, "What we do now,

Pawpaw?" Just the sound of his voice makes the sun rise and the world turn.

The laugh of a baby, the whisper of a lover, the commendation of a boss, the marching orders of a general: these touch the soul and transform the spirit; they move nations and change the world. The three-day battle at Gettysburg was important, but the part of that struggle that now echoes around the world are the words that were spoken there five months after the battle ceased: "Four score and seven years ago …" Martin Luther King, Jr. marched all over the country, but it was what he said that reverberates around the world: "I have a dream."

Your voice matters. Do not fear to use your voice for the glory of God and the gospel of Jesus Christ our Lord.

A few years ago I had a student, a talented, dedicated student. He came to college as a ministerial student, a preacher boy. After a year or so he was ready to give up preaching. "I want to run the sound board," he said to me one day. "And what would really invigorate our campus worship are smoke machines." He then submitted a lengthy, detailed proposal for better sound effects and more smoke.

I wanted to shake him. As a matter of fact, I think I did shake him. He had the ability to stand in front of people and declare the good news of God, but he had drifted into a vocational fog. Screens and smoke will never replace one person standing face to face with one person, or one thousand people, and speaking with intelligence and passion.

Do not be afraid of your voice. When you speak, the fire of God burns bright. When you speak, the fire in your soul ignites the mind and imagination of another. When you speak, you become like Jeremiah and like Jesus, the power of God; the fire in your bones dances across time and space to melt the heart, purge the soul, and set on fire the holy imagination of those who listen.

When the youthful Jeremiah was hesitant to own his voice and unloose his speech for the glory of God, here is what happened: "Then the Lord put out a hand and touched my mouth and said, 'I have put my words in your mouth'" (1:9).

Use your voice to declare the good news of God. Do not fear what God has called you to do. God will give you words and use these words coming out of your heart and lips to set the world on fire! Do not be afraid of your voice!

God used another set of images to describe Jeremiah's vocation as a public preacher. "You will plant and pluck. You will build up and tear down. You will create and destroy" (1:10).

God understood what some of you do not: The spoken word has power to change things, to transform human life, to make a difference in the world.

This entire preaching movement, this whole Academy of Preachers, this National Festival of Young Preachers arose out of the soil of indecision, out of a field of doubt, out of the harvest of hesitation. Too many college students in my care had lost confidence that preaching is a socially significant vocation. They, like you, love Jesus and want to make a difference in the world. They, like you, want to live lives of significance. But they were not convinced that the preaching voice is a fulcrum by which you can move the world. So they explored careers in law, and public service, and education, and social justice. These all are vocations of honor and worth. But the human voice that speaks with passion and eloquence, lifting the horizons of hope and parting the waters of despair, that voice will shape the future of human life on this planet.

Time magazine produced a list last year of the 100 most influential people in the world. Some on the list you would expect: presidents, politicians, managers, tycoons, judges, artists, writers, inventors. One category is omitted: preachers. Yes, there is one nun, who runs a charity. Not a preacher, prophet, or pastor on the list!

Not a single reference to those people who speak into the public square the gospel word; who organize people to serve, sacrifice, and volunteer; who offer words of encouragement to people burdened by grief, anger, confusion, and failure; who call a congregation to clothe the naked, visit the lonely, welcome the stranger; who announce the forgiveness of sins and the hope of eternal life; who teach the most significant book ever written; who critique every earthly empire and contend for the kingdom of God; who direct the most powerful dramas on Earth, around this table and in the pool back there; who declare, the time is fulfilled, and today is the day of salvation; who confess to themselves and to God, "There is something like a fire shut up in my bones; I am weary from holding it in and I cannot."

Do not fear your vocation, young preacher. Do not doubt its power. Jesus came preaching, not because there were no other avenues of influence, but because the voice touches the soul, and the voice dancing with the fire of God singes the soul of the world.

The most influential person in the world when I was your age was not a politician, not a general, not a lawyer, not an entertainer, certainly not an athlete. He was a teacher and a preacher, living in exile, recording his words on cassette tapes and mailing them all over the world. He fomented a revolution, what we now call the Islamic revolution. He was the Ayatollah Khomeini. He challenged the power and culture of the United States and all the western world. He had a moral vision of human life on planet Earth. He was a preacher. He shook the world. The vibrations still shaking the world were set in motion by the force and fury of his words.

"A word is dead when it is said, some say," and here I quote the lady of Amherst, "I say, it just begins to live that day."

Your words have unlimited power to bring salvation and redemption, to call people and nations to righteousness and justice, and to announce that the kingdoms of this world have become the kingdoms of our Lord and of our Christ.

God has set a fire in your bones! God has ignited your soul. There is among us: another

Desmond Tutu, ready to lead a nation toward reconciliation; another John Paul, turning east to rebuke atheism and turning west to condemn materialism; another Billy Graham, globetrotting the world to declare the word of God; another Martin Luther King, Jr. lifting the whole world with a dream of inclusion and cooperation; another Sharon Watkins, standing before the nations and calling a president to lead his people with moral courage.

Do not fear your youth. This is the time when God ignites the fire. Do not fear your voice. It is the power of God to declare the unsearchable riches of Jesus Christ. Do not fear your vocation. It is the purpose of God in your life and in the world.

If you live and speak without fear, someone will say of you, "He reminds me of Jeremiah" and "She reminds me of Jesus." You will have fulfilled your vocation. And one day, you will receive your reward. Not a cathedral or a palace or a throne, but something said and something spoken. Not a retirement package or a title or a crown, but God the righteous judge will speak to you the only words that matter: "Well done, good and faithful servant."

Academy of Preachers

The Academy of Preachers (AoP) is a national, non-profit, trans-denominational organization with a mission to "identify, network, support, and inspire young people in the call to gospel preaching." It was launched in 2009 by Dwight A. Moody with a generous grant from the Lilly Endowment of Indianapolis, Indiana. Dr. Moody continues to serve as president of the AoP. The AoP is undergirded by the conviction that gospel preaching is a socially significant vocation worthy of the very best and brightest of our young adults.

The Academy of Preachers publishes each year a selection of the sermons from the annual National Festival of Young Preachers. To date, these books include *A Beautiful Thing* (2010), *Waking to the Holy* (2011), *Uncommon Sense* (2012), *Gospel and the City* (2013), and *Tell Me a Story* (2014), all published by Chalice Press; two other volumes of sermons are in production. The preaching theme for 2015, including the National Festival in January of 2016, is HEAVEN & EARTH.

For more information about the Academy of Preachers, including how you can join the AoP as a Young Preacher, Professional Minister, or iPartner, please consult one of these avenues of information:

Academy of Preachers
150 East High Street
Lexington, Kentucky 40507
859-533-9929
academyofpreachers.net
youtube.com/academyofpreachers